RESTORING THE DIVINE PARTICIPATION

The Holy Spirit's Role and The Path To True Repentance

SAMEH SAIED

LOGOS ECHOES

CONTENTS

Part Three
True Repentance Unveiled:
From Self-Love to Christ-Centred Renewal

But when he, the Spirit of truth, comes,
he will guide you into all the truth.
He will not speak on his own;
he will speak only what he hears,
and he will tell you what is yet to come.
He will glorify me because it is from me
that he will receive what he will make known
to you.

John 16:13-14

PREFACE

God's Invisible Presence:
Experiencing the Transformative Power of the
Holy Spirit

Though we cannot see God with our physical eyes, His presence is undeniably felt around us. We have an innate awareness of His surrounding presence, as Paul the Apostle described: "*For since the creation of the world, God's invisible qualities—his eternal power and divine nature—have been clearly seen, being understood from what has been made*" (Rom.1:19-20). This deep awareness allows us to communicate with Him, seek His guidance, and hear His voice resonate within our souls. Even if we do not see Him physically, we engage with a living presence that fills our lives like a light dispelling darkness. In prayer, we address Him as "*Our Father in heaven*" (Matt. 6:9), read His Word in the Scriptures, and come to understand His ways.

The profound reality of God became even more tangible with the incarnation of the Word—Jesus Christ, the only Son. Jesus is "*the radiance of God's glory and the exact representation of his being*" (Heb.1:3), the image of the invisible God (Col.1:15). Jesus affirmed, "*Anyone who has seen me has seen the Father*" (John 14:9). The Apostle John desired to share this vivid experience with us: "*That which we have heard, which we have seen with our eyes, which we have looked at and our hands have touched—this we proclaim concerning the Word of life... We proclaim to you what we have seen and heard, so that you also may have fellowship with us"* (1 John 1:1-3). This relationship enables us to engage personally with Jesus, loving, seeking, and feeling His closeness as He embraced our human nature.

But What about our connection with the third person of the Holy Trinity, the Holy Spirit? Few grasp His role in our lives, particularly in our spiritual journey. Even fewer actively seek a relationship with Him or experience His work. Most of us only interact with the Holy Spirit through church prayers, and some might not even recognize His presence while reciting these prayers. This could be due to a limited understanding of the Holy Spirit and His role, as well as a failure to pursue a direct relationship with Him. Just as the Church is united with Christ, acknowledging His leadership and sacrificial love, it is also united with the Holy Spirit, fully aware of its dependence on Him. Therefore, we must recognize the Holy Spirit's role in both our personal and communal lives and build a strong personal connection with Him.

The Holy Spirit is the Spirit of God, the Spirit of Christ, the very essence of Christ's mind, and the Lord Himself. He embodies wisdom, understanding, counsel, might, knowledge, godliness, and fear of the Lord. He permeates the world with His essence without being confined by it. He is good, righteous, and sanctifies by nature, not by adoption. He measures but is not measured, participates but is not shared, fills but is not filled, contains but is not contained, and takes inheritance. He is glorified with the Father and the Son and acts as the agent of promise. He is the finger of God, a fire like God. As the Creator Spirit, He renews creation through baptism and resurrection. He knows all things, teaches as He wills, speaks, discerns, illuminates, and imparts life—He is light and life. He shapes us into

His temples, completing us, and pre-empting and seeking after baptism. He performs all that God does, distributing gifts, and making apostles, prophets, evangelists, pastors, and teachers. His understanding is comprehensive, penetrating, and incorruptible, all-powerful, all-seeing, and applies to all understanding spirits, pure as with the prophets and apostles. This demonstrates the limitless nature of the Holy Spirit.

On a personal level, the Holy Spirit is known as the Spirit of grace, the source of all goodness and virtue. He embodies wisdom in Solomon, knowledge in Bezalel, counsel in Moses, strength in Joshua, piety in Tobiah, understanding in Daniel, and fear of God in Simeon. The Holy Spirit guides us toward eternal life, teaching integrity and providing support. If we falter, He helps us overcome sin and prevents our downfall. He is the Comforter in sorrow, light in darkness, advocate in distress, saviour in trouble, counsellor in doubt, sweetness in bitterness, strength in weakness, guide in error, and teacher in ignorance. These are the gifts the Holy Spirit continually bestows upon believers. Just as a sailboat cannot complete its journey smoothly without the wind, despite its equipment, we need the grace of the Holy Spirit to navigate the present life and reach eternal life.

The Holy Spirit plays a crucial role in our repentance and spiritual growth. We must pay close attention to our spiritual struggle against sin and the world, recognizing that any effort not grounded in the faith of the Holy Spirit is in vain. We must trust that Christ does not work in us without the Holy Spirit, and the Holy Spirit does not work in us without Christ. Similarly, we cannot accomplish anything without both Christ and the Holy Spirit. The Holy Spirit takes from Christ and gives to us, with the remarkable ability to receive everything that belongs to Christ and impart it to us.

With His transcendent power over human nature, intellect, and body, the Holy Spirit undertakes the task of breaking the law of sin and shattering the dominion of death over human nature through a profound, sacramental process. This involves replacing our old human life with the life of the living Christ. The Holy Spirit utilizes our steadfast faith in the living Christ, and through this faith, He penetrates the depths of human intellect and will, leading them to align with Christ's thoughts and will. This initiates a comprehensive transformation, empowering the individual to fight against sin with a new strength beyond their previous intellectual and volitional capacities.

On-going spiritual growth and the struggle against sin are not a matter of human will or personal ambition but are, in truth, sincere obedience to the Holy Spirit's guidance. Once a person accepts the Holy Spirit and submits to His counsel, authority, and light, they are empowered to perform good deeds, which are considered righteous as if from their own will and faith. Without the Holy Spirit, we remain lost and distant from the Father's love and the Son's grace, lacking redemption, salvation, adoption, and hope.

To truly become a dwelling place and throne for God, the human soul must be ignited by the fire of the Holy Spirit. This transformation enables it to undertake all good works and bold acts of faith and witness. The soul's insight must be fully opened to understand all things of God, becoming as if it were all-seeing and illuminated. The Holy Spirit's work in the human soul is of utmost importance and precision, and it must be complete in every way for the soul to be worthy of God's dwelling.

Introduction

In an era where the hustle and clamour of modern life often obscure the whispers of the divine, the quest for genuine spiritual connection is more pressing than ever. *"Restoring The Divine Participation: The Holy Spirit's Role and the Path to True Repentance"* stands as a beacon for those seeking to rediscover a vibrant, transformative relationship with the Divine.

This book invites you on an illuminating journey to explore the profound and dynamic role of the Holy Spirit in our spiritual lives. It is not merely an academic discussion but a heartfelt call to revitalize our engagement with the sacred, bridging the gap between the transcendent and the everyday. We delve into how the Holy Spirit serves as the vital conduit, guiding us through the often challenging but ultimately rewarding path of true repentance and spiritual renewal.

Within these pages, you will uncover how the Holy Spirit is not an abstract concept but a personal, intimate presence that interacts with our innermost struggles and aspirations. Through this exploration, we will reveal the essence of repentance — not just as a ritualistic act but as a profound, transformative journey that reshapes every aspect of our being.

"Restoring The Divine Participation" seeks to reignite a passion for spiritual depth, illustrating how the Holy Spirit's role is central to our journey of repentance. This book challenges you to move beyond superficial spirituality and engage in a deeper, more authentic connection with God. It offers

a fresh perspective on repentance as a gateway to a more profound, Christ-centred life.

With this book, You will find not only theological insights but also practical wisdom for nurturing a genuine relationship with the Holy Spirit. "*Restoring The Divine Participation*" is more than a guide—it is an invitation to rediscover and restore the divine spark within you, leading to a path of spiritual renewal and fulfilment.

In this pivotal part of our book, we embark on an in-depth journey to uncover the profound and transformative presence of the Holy Spirit within us, exploring its eternal significance in both body and spirit. Titled "*The Holy Spirit Within Us: Understanding Its Eternal Presence in Body and Spirit*," this segment is dedicated to revealing the depth and breadth of the Holy Spirit's influence and its critical role in our spiritual and physical lives.

Our exploration begins with "*The Presence of the Holy Spirit Within Us*," where we lay the foundation for understanding the profound impact of the Holy Spirit on our existence. This section aims to illuminate how the Holy Spirit's indwelling transcends mere theological concepts, touching every facet of our daily lives and spiritual journey. It introduces the reader to the transformative power of the Spirit, setting the stage for a deeper comprehension of its workings.

Following this, "*The Presence of the Holy Spirit in the Body*" delves into the intricate relationship between the Spirit and our physical form. This section examines how the Holy Spirit sanctifies and inhabits our bodies, highlighting the divine integration of spirit and flesh. It provides insights into how the Spirit's presence can influence our physical well-being and how recognizing this connection can enhance our spiritual practice.

In "*How Do We Discern the Presence of the Holy Spirit in the Body?*" we address the practical aspect of identifying and interpreting the manifestations of the Spirit within our physical selves. This section offers practical tools and spiritual discernment techniques to help readers recognize the subtle and profound ways in which the Holy Spirit is at work in their lives, fostering a deeper awareness and connection with the divine presence.

Our journey then takes us to "*Do Not Judge the Body as Evil*," where we confront and challenge the prevalent misconceptions about the physical body as inherently flawed or sinful. This section emphasizes the inherent goodness and divine purpose of the body, encouraging readers to embrace their physical selves as integral to their spiritual journey.

"*Does the Holy Spirit Depart When We Sin?*" addresses a critical question concerning the relationship between divine presence and human imperfection. This section provides reassurance and theological clarity on the continuous presence of the Holy Spirit, even amidst our moral failures and struggles, emphasizing the Spirit's role as a constant guide and source of grace.

In "*The Eternal Presence of the Holy Spirit in Us*," we explore the unchanging and steadfast nature of the Holy Spirit's presence. This section offers comfort and stability, reinforcing the idea that the Holy Spirit remains with us through all phases of our spiritual lives, providing a source of divine support and encouragement.

We then explore "*The Indwelling of the Holy Spirit and the Promise of Resurrection*," connecting the presence of the Spirit with the profound hope of eternal life. This section highlights how the Holy Spirit prepares us for resurrection, bridging the gap between our current existence and the promise of eternal life with God.

"The Impact of Sin on the Body and Spirit: Understanding the Dichotomy" investigates how sin affects both our physical and spiritual dimensions. This section offers a nuanced exploration of the impact of sin, examining how it creates a divide between body and spirit and discussing ways to address and heal this rift.

"Alienation of the Body from the Spirit" addresses the challenges that arise when there is a disconnection between our physical and spiritual selves. This section examines the causes of this alienation and offers insights into restoring harmony and unity between body and spirit.

Finally, *"The Divine Love for Sinners and the Promise of Renewal"* celebrates the boundless love of God for all humanity, emphasizing the continuous promise of renewal and redemption offered through the Holy Spirit. This section underscores the Spirit's role in facilitating our spiritual growth, healing, and ultimate reconciliation with God.

Through this part, we aim to provide a comprehensive and engaging exploration of the Holy Spirit's role in our lives. Each section is crafted to offer profound insights, practical guidance, and spiritual inspiration, helping readers experience the transformative power of the Holy Spirit and its eternal presence in every aspect of their being. We invite you to journey with us through these pages, discovering the profound depths of divine presence and the boundless possibilities for spiritual renewal and growth.

In the second part of our book, *"From Spiritual Death to Eternal Life: Sin, Repentance, Divine Justice, and the Promise of Resurrection."* Building upon the foundational themes established in the first part, this part delves profoundly into the critical journey from spiritual death to the promise of eternal life. It addresses pivotal aspects of Christian theology, exploring the intricate dynamics of sin, repentance, divine justice, and the ultimate hope of resurrection with depth and clarity.

Our exploration begins with "*Understanding Sin and Redemption,*" where we lay a comprehensive foundation for grasping the nature of sin and the profound process of redemption. This section provides essential insights into the transformative power of divine forgiveness and sets the stage for the transformative journey that lies ahead.

In "*Spiritual Death and Hell: Two Sides of the Same Coin,*" we navigate the complex relationship between spiritual death and the concept of hell, shedding light on how these concepts intersect and influence one another within Christian thought. This section provides a nuanced understanding of the consequences of spiritual death and the nature of hell, paving the way for deeper theological reflection.

We then turn our focus to "*Jesus and the Restoration of Life,*" which examines how Christ's sacrifice and resurrection provide the pathway from spiritual death to new life. This section highlights the central role of Jesus in overcoming the separation from God and restoring spiritual vitality, offering profound insights into the significance of His redemptive work.

The inquiry continues with "*Is Spiritual Death a Separation from God?*" addressing the nature of spiritual estrangement and its impact on our relationship with the divine. This section explores whether spiritual death constitutes a complete separation from God or if it reflects a more nuanced state of spiritual distance.

"*Signs of Separation from God and Spiritual Death*" offers practical guidance for recognizing the indicators of spiritual estrangement. It provides readers with valuable tools to identify and address the signs of spiritual death in their own lives and the lives of those around them. Similarly, "*An Example of Spiritual Death on Earth*" illustrates real-world manifestations of spiritual death, offering tangible examples to help readers relate these concepts to their everyday experiences.

We then delve into "*The Authority of Satan and Genuine Repentance,*" examining the adversarial role of Satan and its implications for true repentance. This section explores the nature of genuine repentance and how it contrasts with mere superficial contrition, emphasizing the importance of authentic spiritual transformation.

"*Indicators of Genuine Repentance*" provides a framework for recognizing true repentance, offering practical insights into the signs of a sincere and transformative change of heart. This section guides readers in understanding how genuine repentance manifests in their lives and in the lives of others.

In "*The Meaning of Christ's Wounds and the Hope of Resurrection,*" we explore the profound significance of Christ's suffering and its implications for our hope in resurrection. This section highlights how Christ's wounds symbolize both His sacrificial love and the promise of new life for all who believe.

"*Triumph Over Death and the Mystery of Final Renewal*" examines the ultimate victory over death and the profound mystery of final renewal. This section offers a hopeful perspective on the eschatological promise of resurrection and the transformative power of Christ's victory over death.

Addressing the complexities of suffering and mortality, "*How Did the Lord Remove the Curse of Death, and Why Do We Still Die and Are Buried?*" explores theological questions about the nature of death and the reasons for on-going human mortality despite Christ's redemptive work. "*Why Does Renewal Await the Final Day?*" further examines why the complete renewal of creation is deferred until the final day, providing insights into the eschatological vision of Christianity.

"Understanding the Path to Redemption: The Role of Discipline, Grace, and Spiritual Growth" provides a comprehensive view of the journey towards redemption, highlighting the roles of spiritual discipline, divine grace, and personal growth. This chapter emphasizes how these elements interact to facilitate spiritual transformation and renewal.

In *"Understanding the Grace of Baptism and the Nature of Sin,"* we explore the sacrament of baptism as a transformative act of grace and its role in addressing the nature of sin. This section delves into the theological significance of baptism and its impact on the believer's journey.

"Understanding Divine Justice" and *"Understanding the Concept of Hell in Christian Theology"* offer in-depth analyses of divine justice and the theological understanding of hell. These sections clarify critical aspects of Christian doctrine, providing readers with a deeper appreciation of God's justice and the nature of eternal punishment.

"The Divine Mystery of the Son's Self-Emptying" reveals the profound theological concept of kenosis, or Christ's self-emptying, and its implications for our understanding of divine love and humility. *"Understanding the Nature of Evil and Its Resolution in Christ"* addresses the problem of evil and its resolution through the redemptive work of Christ, offering a comprehensive view of how evil is confronted and overcome.

"The Return to the Self: A Path to Spiritual Rebirth" and *"The Cross as the Path to Spiritual Enlightenment"* focus on personal spiritual transformation, exploring how the journey back to the self and the cross lead to profound spiritual enlightenment and rebirth. These sections emphasize

the role of individual transformation in the broader context of Christian faith.

Finally, *"The Enduring Image of God and the Power of Spiritual Unity," "Unity in the Church: A Divine Gift and Collective Responsibility," "The Cross as the Law of Love," "The Role of Discernment in Love,"* and *"The Essential Role of Service in Spiritual Growth"* tie together the themes of divine image, unity, love, discernment, and service. These sections underscore the importance of spiritual unity and the practical expressions of love and service as essential components of spiritual growth.

Through this second part of our book, we aim to offer a profound and engaging exploration of the journey from spiritual death to eternal life. Each section provides theological insights, practical guidance, and spiritual inspiration, designed to deepen your understanding and foster a renewed commitment to spiritual growth and transformation. We invite you to delve into these pages and discover the transformative power of faith and the promise of eternal life.

The third part of our comprehensive exploration, *"True Repentance Unveiled: From Self-Love to Christ-Centred Renewal."* In this pivotal Part, we advance beyond the foundational themes laid out in the previous parts to delve into the intricate dynamics of genuine repentance. Here, we uncover the path from self-centred existence to a life transformed by Christ, highlighting the essential elements and divine grace that underpin true spiritual renewal.

We commence with *"True Repentance: The Necessity of Genuine Love,"* setting the stage for a deep understanding of authentic repentance. This section emphasizes that true repentance is fundamentally rooted in a profound, genuine love — for God, for oneself, and for others. It is this love that catalyses the transformative process necessary for true spiritual change and renewal.

Moving forward, *"The Path to True Repentance: Moving Beyond Self-Love"* charts the critical transition from self-centeredness to a Christ-centred perspective. Here, we explore the necessary steps to shift from a focus on self-love to embracing a life devoted to Christ. This section offers practical insights and spiritual guidance for navigating this transformative journey.

"Repentance: The Gateway to New Life in Christ" illuminates how repentance serves as the essential entryway to a new existence in Christ. This section demonstrates how the act of genuine repentance not only facilitates a renewed relationship with God but also leads to a deeper, more fulfilling spiritual life.

The role of the Holy Spirit is further examined in *"The Role of the Holy Spirit in True Repentance,"* where we uncover how the Holy Spirit empowers and guides believers through the process of repentance. This section highlights the Spirit's crucial role in facilitating genuine change and fostering a closer walk with Christ.

In *"The Death of Sin: Rejection of Grace and Denial of Christ,"* we confront the gravity of sin as an outright rejection of divine grace and a denial of Christ's redemptive work. This section explores the severe consequences of sin and underscores the necessity of embracing grace to overcome its effects.

"The Divine Gift Preserved by the Holy Trinity" reveals the profound truth that the gift of repentance and renewal is upheld and cherished by the Holy Trinity. This section explores how the Father, Son, and Holy Spirit collaboratively sustain and nurture the divine gift of repentance, ensuring its transformative power.

We then delve into *"Understanding True Humility and the Role of Confession in Spiritual Renewal,"* which highlights the significance of humility in the repentance process. This section explores how true humility opens the door to spiritual healing and renewal through the practice of confession, fostering a deeper connection with God.

"The Role of Confession in Spiritual Healing" provides a closer look at how confession acts as a vital instrument in spiritual recovery. This section offers practical advice on embracing confession as a means of healing and growth, facilitating a more profound relationship with Christ.

"Discerning the Intentions of the Heart" emphasizes the importance of understanding one's true motives in the repentance journey. This section encourages introspection and self-awareness to ensure that repentance is not merely superficial but genuinely transformative.

Finally, *"Living Under the Grace of Christ: Embracing True Purity and Understanding the Role of the Psalms"* integrates the themes of grace and purity with practical spiritual practice. This section demonstrates how living under the grace of Christ leads to true purity and explores how the Psalms can enrich and support spiritual growth.

In this third part of our book, we aim to offer a thorough and engaging examination of true repentance and spiritual renewal. Each section provides deep theological insights, practical guidance, and spiritual inspiration, designed to enhance your understanding and support your journey towards a life centred on Christ. We invite you to immerse yourself in these pages and experience the transformative power of genuine repentance and divine grace.

The Presence of the Holy Spirit Within Us

When we discuss the indwelling of the Holy Spirit, we are exploring a core aspect of our spiritual existence that deeply influences our lives. We live with the hope of being renewed through the power of the Cross and Resurrection, and by the grace of the Holy Spirit given to us in Holy Baptism, which we receive directly from the Lord Himself. The Holy Spirit sanctifies and completes every ministry within the Holy Church.

The humility of the Holy Spirit is truly remarkable. He imparts life to our bodies, even though they are destined to die. The Holy Spirit, as the gentle Spirit of Life, bestows the gift of vitality on all things. He breathes life into flowers and plants, stirs the air, enriches the soil so that it can produce crops, and leads all creation towards life. Through His boundless grace, He gives existence and vitality, allowing all creation to praise the Lord—the Giver of goodness and life. Both heaven and earth join in glorifying the Holy Trinity: the Father, the Son, and the Holy Spirit.

The Apostle Paul tells us that the Lord Jesus will safeguard "*His deposit until that day*," referring to the Day of Judgment. This deposit encompasses both soul and body. The soul receives spiritual life directly from the Holy Spirit, who is the "*breath of life.*" This was confirmed by Jesus when He breathed on His disciples after His resurrection, restoring to them the breath of life as described in the Gospel of John. It is not difficult to understand that the Holy Spirit engages with the soul or human spirit at an unseen, spiritual level through His divine power, guiding the human spirit towards holiness, love, and the freedom of the glory of the children of God. However, discussing the body presents a challenge for several reasons.

Firstly, it is difficult to describe the Holy Spirit in a visible way, while the body is visible, tangible, and limited. Yet this challenge is eased when we remember that the human body is the visible aspect of the human spirit. Every movement and function of the body originates from the human spirit, which derives its life from the Holy Spirit. For instance, when I write, my hand moves because of my will, which is guided by the spirit. While words are visible, their meanings are unseen, though understood by both of us.

Secondly, the Holy Spirit anoints the human spirit and transfers to the body the power and gifts of the only Son. The mortal and perishable human body, which returns to the earth's dust, unites with Christ in baptism to live and rise again on the last day, as promised by the Lord in the sixth chapter of the Gospel of John. Thus, we experience divine life even while we are *"living in the land of death and its shadows."* The light of the glory of the Lord Jesus shines upon us until the day we are freed from the *"body of death,"* which has not yet attained resurrection.

The Presence of the Holy Spirit in the Body

At this point in our reflection, it is crucial to address a fundamental question: How does the Holy Spirit dwell within the human body? To fully understand this, we need to explore several essential points:

1. *Understanding the Nature of the Body*: The human body is not merely a physical entity defined by measurements such as size and shape. In the context of sin and evil, the body has been reduced to a set of quantifiable attributes like "*size, shape, colour, type, and dimensions.*" However, the body is fundamentally a divine gift from God the Father. This gift has been sanctified and transformed into an eternal blessing through the Incarnation of the Son, who took on human flesh from the Virgin Mary and rose from the dead in that very same body. The body's original divine purpose and its ultimate sanctity are revealed through this sacred union with the divine.

2. *The Body as the Manifestation of the Human Spirit*: The body should be viewed through a spiritual lens rather than merely through physical desires and appetites. In a world tainted by sinful desires, physical attributes such as size and possession often become the standards by which we judge value and worth. Sinful perspectives focus on visible attributes like weight, length, and width, which are associated with ownership and control. In contrast, holiness evaluates what is

true and pure, transcending superficial metrics. Jesus instructs us not to despise what appears small or weak. These elements, though seemingly insignificant by worldly standards, hold equal value in spiritual terms. The Apostle Paul, for instance, emphasizes that women, often perceived as weaker by societal standards, are "*co-heirs of the grace of life*" and deserving of love as Christ loves the Church. This spiritual perspective challenges us to move beyond mere appearances and embrace the true value bestowed by God.

3. *Spiritual Perception and Sanctification of the Body*: Since the body represents the visible aspect of the human spirit, it must be perceived spiritually through the lens of the Holy Spirit's sanctifying power. We should avoid favouring certain parts of the body or judging its beauty based on superficial traits. Instead, when the Holy Spirit sanctifies a person's heart, the entire body becomes a sacred temple, reflecting the sacred spaces of the Tabernacle: the Holy of Holies, the altar, the outer court, the laver, and the altar of incense. The Incarnation of Jesus Christ imbued the human body with divine significance, transforming it into a temple of the divine presence.

4. *The Body as the Venue for Divine Presence in the World*: The body serves as the dwelling place of the human spirit in this world, and thus, it is also a venue for the revelation of the Holy Trinity. Jesus taught that those who love Him will have Him come to them and make His home with them, indicating that human beings, in their entirety — body and

spirit—are the dwelling place of the Trinity. Therefore, it is imperative to sanctify this temple, as it is the only place through which the light of the Holy Spirit shines and operates within the community. Historically, the Holy Spirit has visibly anointed kings, judges, and prophets, and on the Day of Pentecost, He manifested as tongues of fire upon the disciples. Through this anointing, the apostles performed divine works— healing, proclamation, and exorcism—by the power of the Holy Spirit. Even objects like handkerchiefs and aprons from St. Paul were used to drive out demons and heal the sick, showing that material objects can also partake in the Holy Spirit's sanctifying grace. The Holy Spirit sanctifies not just the invisible, but also the visible and material aspects of creation, revealing the glory of the Holy Trinity.

5. *The Unique Status of the Human Body Through the Incarnation*: When the Lord was incarnated from the Virgin Mary, He conferred upon the human body a unique status that it had not possessed before. First, all revelations of salvation were accomplished through the body of the Lord, which accepted divine humility by assuming the form of a servant. Second, His ultimate act of love was demonstrated through His sacrifice on the cross, where He defeated death and broke its power, and through His resurrection, He promised eternal life. Thus, the Lord's body became the focal point of divine revelation and salvation, embodying *"the fullness of the Godhead bodily"* (Col.2:9).

The anointing of the Son by the Holy Spirit transformed Christ into an invisible, spiritual anointing. This enabled Him to offer His body on the cross with the power of the eternal Spirit, as stated by the Apostle (Heb. 9:14). This act unified the work of the Holy Spirit with the priestly service of Christ, making the cross a source of life that overcomes death and nullifies the curse of the law (Gal.3:13). By offering His body through the Holy Spirit, Christ established the Spirit as a co-worker in the work of salvation, merging the divine life of the Spirit with the cross. This is why the sign of the cross is used in our prayers—it represents the seal of the Holy Trinity, through which we sanctify and complete our spiritual service.

When Jesus rose with divine power, He united the work of the Holy Spirit with the resurrection, declaring that He was raised by the Spirit (Rom.8:11). Consequently, our resurrection is not only due to Christ's resurrection but also because of the unity in the divine plan of salvation. The Spirit received the power of resurrection from Christ to grant us this power as an inheritance, enabling us to experience the glory of resurrection on the last day. Thus, the act of sacrifice becomes a power of sanctification that triumphs over death and is imparted to us in our prayers, especially in the sacrament of Holy Baptism. We pray that those baptized in the name of the Holy Trinity become spiritual sacrifices, as the Apostle Paul instructs us to offer our bodies as living sacrifices to God the Father in spiritual worship, in spirit and truth.

How Do We Discern the Presence of the Holy Spirit in the Body?

To fully grasp the presence of the Holy Spirit in the body, we must first understand that the Holy Spirit dwells within the human soul. Because humans are an integrated unity of body and soul, the Spirit's presence extends from the soul to the body. This unity implies that the way the Spirit interacts with the soul is also reflected in the body. Here's how the Holy Spirit's presence in the soul manifests in the body:

1. *In Perception*: The Holy Spirit enlightens our understanding by opening the eyes of our soul to perceive spiritual truths. This divine insight allows us to see beyond the physical world and grasp the deeper, often hidden, realities of God's kingdom. This spiritual perception transforms our view of the world and guides us toward truth and understanding.

2. *In the Heart*: The Holy Spirit fills our heart with a fervent love for Jesus. This love is characterized by a profound attachment and commitment, even in the face of trials or threats. The Spirit ensures that our devotion remains steadfast, regardless of life's challenges, and sustains our love for Christ through difficult circumstances.

3. *In the Will*: The Holy Spirit influences our will, prompting us to engage in prayer, self-denial, and active love for Jesus. This guidance helps us to live with a hopeful expectation of future glory and to act with a

purpose aligned with God's will. The Spirit's influence directs our choices and actions, driving us to live in a way that reflects our faith and hope in God's promises.

Given that the Holy Spirit dwells in the mind, heart, and will, the next question is how this spiritual presence extends to the body. The body serves as the visible manifestation of the spirit. Every physical action and movement is energized by the life force received from the union with the soul. We can experience the Holy Spirit's influence in our physical state in several ways. For instance, when we experience spiritual renewal and joy, physical needs such as hunger, fatigue, or lack of sleep may seem less significant. This divine presence often provides us with strength and resilience beyond our usual capacity, especially when we engage in acts of service or face physical challenges.

Many believers have observed that during fasting or extended periods of physical deprivation, the body remains unexpectedly at ease and content. This phenomenon illustrates the Holy Spirit's presence in the body, as it provides a sense of peace and well-being even in the absence of physical sustenance.

It is crucial to understand that physical exhaustion, lack of sleep, or illness should not be interpreted as signs that the Holy Spirit has departed from us. Such experiences are part of human vulnerability and weakness. The Lord reassured Paul, *"My grace is sufficient for you, for my power is made perfect in weakness"* (2 Cor. 12:9). This affirmation means that physical difficulties do not equate to the Holy Spirit's absence but rather highlight our reliance on divine grace.

As devoted believers striving for spiritual completeness and glory in Christ Jesus, we must declare and affirm that God's gifts and grace are not withdrawn due to our sins. Instead, these gifts are given to sinners, reflecting God's desire to uphold them through His Son, our Lord Jesus Christ. If our conscience or heart accuses us of failing to live up to God's promises, such accusations may stem from our old nature or from the devil. The old nature is not a real entity post-baptism but consists of lingering memories and past experiences that resurface from time to time. We continue to live in a world that has received a pledge of redemption through Jesus Christ but is not yet fully redeemed. As Paul writes, *"The whole creation groans and labours with birth pangs"* (Rom.8:22), awaiting the final renewal. We are complete in God, but apart from Him, we are flawed and sinful. In Christ, we are glorified, but without Him, we face ruin. We are children of God by grace but remain servants by nature. Christ stands at the door and knocks, affirming His unchanging love and unwavering commitment to what He has given us. Trust that you remain secure in God's mercy, as the Apostle assures that God's gifts and calling are *"irrevocable"* (Rom.11:29).

Despite being burdened by the flesh, and mistakenly believing that the body is the source of sin and conflict due to spiritual ignorance, we must remember that, according to divine teaching, the body's actions are driven by the will. The will, in turn, is influenced by the mind, which operates through free choice. This process of human action is often constrained by hidden desires and unconscious longings. The human heart is a vast vessel that can contain either the entire world or the Holy Trinity. Here, we speak not of physical size but of the nature of what is contained. Just as a small piece of gold has the same value as a larger piece because it is of the same metal, so too in the Kingdom of God, greatness is not determined by size but by service and giving.

The greatest is the one who serves and gives, embodying the Holy Trinity's boundless ability to bestow and sustain blessings.

Spiritual warfare often begins with subtle, hidden desires that move through the heart, sometimes remaining unnoticed until they manifest strongly within us. These desires might seem to originate from the body or another source, but this is a misunderstanding. All human intentions originate within us, while those implanted by the devil often start as mental or material images, evolving into desires or ideas, and eventually influencing the will. As James explains, *"Each one is tempted when he is drawn away by his own desires and enticed"* (Jam. 1:14). The unity of body and spirit means that thoughts and desires are transferred to the will, leading to actions that are often driven by hidden, intense desires. These desires are influenced by emotions and feelings, as noted in the Psalm: *"Cleanse me from secret faults"* (Ps.19:12). We must remain vigilant, for the Lord warned about the devil sowing tares *"while men slept,"* targeting those who neglect the wisdom of the Holy Spirit.

Do Not Judge the Body as Evil

It is important not to judge the body as evil, for God did not create evil, nor did He create the devil. The devil, originally a cherub, chose to fall from grace. His ambition is captured by the words of the prophet Isaiah: *"I will ascend above the heights of the clouds; I will be like the Most High"* (Is.14:14). This truth must not be forgotten. Nothing is inherently evil in its original state as created by God. According to divine nature and intention, everything is pure and sacred. However, due to the fall and the introduction of sin, everything has adopted a *"non-natural"* form and usage. This is why the Apostle Paul instructs us to *"be transformed by the renewing of your mind"* (Rom.12:2), which involves rediscovering the original nature God intended. Though our actions may become habitual, forming a secondary nature, repentance and the work of the Holy Spirit can restore us to our original state — reflecting the image of God in us. This restoration allows us to inherit the promises of the Lord, making us *"like Him"* in the same glory seen on Mount Transfiguration.

The Holy Spirit dwells in the human soul and extends to the body due to the unity of the person. This unity will be fully restored on the Day of Resurrection, and we experience a foretaste of this life here and now. The Holy Spirit influences the body in three harmonious ways:

1. *Perception of Innocence*: After the fall, our sense of wonder and astonishment often arises from the body's inherent innocence and its non-participation in base thoughts. This feeling comes from the Holy Spirit, who is the Lord of the body and its life-giver. The Spirit restores this sensation to encourage us towards repentance and abandonment of our sins.

2. *Internal Movement*: The Holy Spirit moves the body or some of its parts in an internal manner, sometimes manifesting through sensory or heavenly experiences. These can include visual images of heaven or saints, musical praise, sacred texts, or mental images of loved ones. Such experiences reinforce the soul against sin, highlighting the unity of the human being. The body, as the centre of the visible world, influences deep within the human soul and heart. The Holy Spirit, as the

Lord of the universe and bestower of beauty and glory, moves around us and infuses creation with spiritual significance, bringing comfort, peace, and rest to our souls.

3. *Communion in Prayer:* When we pray, *"Heavenly King, Comforter, Spirit of Truth, who are everywhere and filling all things,"* we unite ourselves—body and soul—with both the visible and invisible realms. The Holy Spirit sanctifies our participation in the cosmic service to our Lord Jesus Christ. The Spirit anoints the body's members with divine grace, reflecting a heart filled with service and kindness. The Holy Spirit teaches both soul and body to stand in *"the position of resurrection,"* symbolizing alertness and readiness. Bodily kneeling signifies submission and originates in the human spirit, while complete prostration represents the voluntary acceptance of death for Jesus, who is always with us in His resurrection power.

The body does not move, nor does even its smallest part, without intention or decision. However, due to the division brought by sin, it is mistakenly believed that the body has its own will. Paul referred to this in his well-known phrases: *"the law of sin in my members"* and *"this body of death"* (Rom.7:23, 24). When the heart is inflamed with desire, it perceives it as an external goal, though desire originates within the heart. When God created us in His image, He provided a foundation for human fellowship. Thus, all our intentions and thoughts involve others externally. Reflect on this: when we think internally, we hear ourselves, and when we hear others, we think. Sometimes, our thoughts intersect with others' thoughts because we were not created for isolation but for communion. Understanding physical behaviour alone, without considering thought and will, is difficult. With the advent of sin, separation due to selfishness emerged, distorting the original intent of fellowship, which became a conflict between a desire for community and isolation. This distortion blinds humans to their need for others, which is essential for complete fellowship and joy. Consequently, Christ became incarnate to share our human existence and establish a new, eternal communion. He experienced physical death, the hidden disease driving sin, but did not experience spiritual death, as He was divine and immortal. He *"suffered once for sins"* (1 Peter3:18), experiencing death with us in the depths of hell, but rose to offer new life that overcomes death and ensures our eternal fellowship in Him, planting the seed of immortal life within us.

Does the Holy Spirit Depart When We Sin?

The question of whether the Holy Spirit departs from us when we sin is one that troubles many believers. This concern is often highlighted by the verse from Psalm 51:11: *"Do not cast me away from Your presence, and do not take Your Holy Spirit from me."* This verse has led some to worry about the possibility of losing the Holy Spirit's presence, especially since we frequently seek the Holy Spirit's presence in our prayers. It is essential to understand that our prayers asking for the Holy Spirit are not about bringing Him to us, but rather about our own need to draw closer to Him. The Holy Spirit came to us on Pentecost and remains with us; it is we who may choose to distance ourselves from Him. The Holy Spirit is unwaveringly faithful, good, and loving, having humbled Himself to dwell within us. In contrast, we are constantly changing because we were created from nothing, and constancy is not our inherent nature. This constant flux is why we call upon the Holy Spirit—to awaken us from spiritual lethargy and to rejuvenate our hearts. When we ask the Father to renew His Holy Spirit within us and not to take Him away, we are committing ourselves to persistent prayer, which is essential to receiving what we seek.

It is crucial to recognize that the indwelling of the Holy Spirit in us, due to the grace of the New Covenant, is fundamentally different from the Holy Spirit's presence with the prophets of the Old Testament. The gift of the Holy Spirit we receive now is greater and more enduring, thanks to the ministry of Jesus Christ, our High Priest. When Jesus was incarnated by the Holy Spirit through the Virgin Mary, He established an eternal foundation for the new birth and restored our fellowship with the Holy Spirit. Jesus Christ, the new and final Adam, or the *"man from heaven"* (1 Cor.15:47), received His human nature from above, from the Spirit of life, to overcome death and its decay.

At His baptism in the Jordan River, Jesus transformed the gift of the Holy Spirit from one of mere life to one of active ministry, encompassing preaching, casting out unclean spirits, healing, forgiving sins, and raising the dead. As the new Adam, Jesus embodied these gifts, and His divine anointing added to the life He received at His birth. He became *"the Christ,"* in whom are hidden all treasures of wisdom and knowledge according to His anointing, and all treasures of life according to His divine nature. The Apostle Paul affirms that Jesus is the guarantor of a better covenant, ensuring that His gifts are perpetual according to the divine promise: *"I will ask the Father, and He will give you another*

Comforter, that He may abide with you forever — the Spirit of Truth whom the world cannot receive because it neither sees Him nor knows Him. But you know Him, for He dwells with you and will be in you" (John.14:16-17). Jesus further reassured us of our fellowship in Him through the Holy Spirit by saying: *"But the Comforter, the Holy Spirit, whom the Father will send in My name, He will teach you all things and bring all things to your remembrance, whatsoever I have said unto you"* (John. 14:26).

He also said: *"I am the vine, and My Father is the vinedresser. Abide in Me, and I in you. As the branch cannot bear fruit of itself unless it abides in the vine, neither can you, unless you abide in Me. I am the vine; you are the branches. He who abides in Me, and I in him, bears much fruit; for without Me, you can do nothing"* (John. 15:1-5). Through these words, Jesus emphasizes that our physical life, or *"special existence,"* is fruitless without Him. Our existence apart from Him is death, reflecting our inherent weakness, as the Apostle Paul confirms (Rom. 8:3). Thus, the Son of God came *"in the likeness of sinful flesh,"* which leads us to personalize the law, making each person the arbiter of good and evil based on their heart's desires.

Jesus lived His earthly life fully integrated with His disciples and with sinners. He embodied the full divine presence of the Father and the Holy Spirit, as He is the incarnate Son, united with the Father and the Holy Spirit. He lived among sinners, dined with hypocrites and adulterers, and demonstrated divine love publicly through His crucifixion. He gave His body in the upper room to those He loved, saying, *"Take, eat; this is My body,"* thus ending the separation between bread and His body. His body became *"the bread of God which comes down from heaven and gives life to the world"* (John.6:33).By unifying His body with the bread, He declared

Himself as the eternal sustenance. He calls us to take up our cross and follow Him, urging us to move beyond our individual existence rooted in sin and embrace a new existence marked by grace. This new existence is derived from fellowship in His body, the Church, and it teaches us to live a new life together, free from the inclinations toward power and dominance that sin corrupts through misuse of material possessions, intellect, and physical abilities.

This is why Jesus established the fundamental law of discipleship: *"deny yourself and take up your cross."* Without self-denial, we cannot live a life of true fellowship because the self is renewed in fellowship, while it remains isolated in sin if not living in communion. Therefore, we must examine ourselves to identify what makes us prefer ourselves over others, particularly in material possessions, food, clothing, money, and even leadership. Conflicts and disputes often reveal selfishness and a desire to assert dominance rather than uphold the commandment of love. Those who impose their views forcefully or enticingly are those who have not recognized themselves as members of the Body of the Lord but see their bodily existence as superior to others.

Even Jesus accepted crucifixion among thieves, showing that His existence is among sinners and evildoers, as He is the Savior who reveals His righteousness and holiness among them. This profound plan is reflected in His name, *"Jesus,"* meaning *"Yahweh saves."* He died among evildoers, saving one of them and bringing him to paradise. Therefore, the Apostle says: *"Casting down imaginations, and every high thing that exalteth itself against the knowledge of God, and bringing into captivity every thought to the obedience of Christ"* (2 Cor.10:5). Through our thoughts, we fall into self-existence but can return to the obedience of the Lord.

The Apostle says: "*Be transformed by the renewing of your mind*" (Rom.12:2). The incarnation of the Son put an end to solitary human existence and established our existence in fellowship within His Body, the Church, as an eternal and everlasting state. After the Lord's incarnation, every person is called to become like the "*Son of Man,*" the new Adam, who, through fellowship in the divine nature, manifests the body in all the glory of Christ through the gifts and blessings of the Holy Spirit, and in the age to come through the manifestation of the Lord Himself, for we shall see Him and become like Him (1 John. 3:2).

The Eternal Presence of the Holy Spirit in Us

The question arises: Does the Holy Spirit remain with us continuously, even when we are engaged in physical activities such as sleeping? The Book of Wisdom tells us, "*The Spirit of the Lord fills the world*" (Wis.7:1). The Apostle Paul expands on this by describing how this divine presence has been renewed with the transformation of creation. He speaks of the Church, which is the body of Christ, as "*the fullness of Him who fills all in all*" (Eph.1:23) and states, "*And you are complete in Him*" (Colo.2:10).

What is this fullness that the wise speak of and that the Evangelist describes as "*full of grace and truth*" (John 1:14)? The Apostle clarifies this by saying, "*For in Him dwells all the fullness of the Godhead bodily*" (Col.2:9). Jesus came embodying the fullness of divine gifts, sent from the Father yet never separated from Him. Born of the Holy Spirit through the Virgin Mary, Jesus brought the fellowship of the Holy Spirit to us through His incarnation, baptism, crucifixion, resurrection, and ascension, "*that He might fill all things*" (Eph.4:10).

In His victory, He "*led captivity captive*" and "*gave gifts to men*" (Eph.4:8), which means He seated us with Him in the heavenly realms. This fulfils the Gospel's message of "*one God and Father of all, who is above all, and through all, and in you all*" (Eph.4:6). This fullness represents communion in the divine nature; it is complete and all-encompassing. As a result, this divine fellowship is available to all believers. Since many enter into the grace of our Lord Jesus Christ, the fullness of humanity is united with the fullness of divinity. This divine fullness is not given to individuals apart from fellowship, as this would contradict the purpose of Christ's incarnation, which was to "*gather together in one the children of God who were scattered abroad*" (John. 11:52).
When Jesus became "*the firstborn among many brethren*" (Rom.8:29), the Holy Spirit dwelled in Him as the Son of Man in a permanent and eternal way.

Even in His final moments, He declared with a loud voice, "*Father, into Your hands I commit My spirit*" (Luke 23:46). As both the sacrifice and the High Priest, He willingly embraced death, overcame it on the cross, and abolished separation entirely. He conquered hell and nullified the power of death— Satan, who had dominion over humanity due to Adam's fall and whom we willingly submit to through temptation and sin.

According to the belief of the holy Church, we affirm that the divinity did not separate from the humanity "*not even for a moment, nor a twinkling of an eye.*" This applies to both the Firstborn and His brethren, as we share in the inheritance of the Lord Jesus. This inheritance was gained through the profound transformation of human relationship with God, moving from the law and ordinances to communion in the divine nature. Despite human weakness and sin, this divine fellowship remains steadfast and eternal in the Head, Jesus Christ our

Lord, and for the members, who are part of His body, of His flesh and of His bones (Eph.5:30).

How does the Lord nourish and nurture His body (Eph.5:29)? How does He love it, having given Himself to purify every member, making all parts of His body glorified in Him, without decay and without the aging of death? We must first recognize an eternal truth: the laws of the first creation mentioned in Genesis do not dominate the new creation. Rather, the new creation is governed by principles given through the holy apostles. The new creation from above is not subject to the laws of the first creation. The Apostle says of the Head of the new creation, *"He has put all things under His feet"* (1 Cor.15:27). This statement, referencing Psalm 8, originally concerned Adam's dominion over the first creation. However, after the fall of the first Adam, the true Adam—the *"Lord from heaven"* (1 Cor.15:47)—established this dominion through the Spirit, using His immense power to bring all things under His authority, creating the new creation in Him, not according to flesh, blood, or human will (John. 1:13).

Though the new creation emerges from the first creation through water, it is by the Spirit and the power that sustains and gives life to all. We must understand that the new creation is in Christ, alive and steadfast, deriving existence from the Father, form from the Son, and eternal life from the Spirit of Life—one work of the Holy Trinity. The new creation surpasses the first creation in three ways: first, in its source; second, in its stability; and third, in its glory and permanence. It originates from God, not from man; it comes from the union of divinity with humanity, not human will; and it is filled with divine goodness and sustained by the power and grace of the Holy Spirit.

Here, the nothingness from which we came has vanished. The source is now divinity, death has been abolished, and we have been given the fullness of fellowship. We are alive to God in Jesus Christ and by the power of the Spirit of Life. Therefore, the laws of the first creation no longer hold dominion over the new creation. Instead, the sovereignty belongs to the Lord, and the authority to the Holy Spirit. Let us draw closer to this profound truth: our original creation from nothing was the cause of our instability. Yet now, our instability is the persistent urge to return to the Lord, the source of life and eternal joy. While we are "*strangers and pilgrims*" in the body, by the Holy Spirit, we are united with Him who has seated us in the heavenly realms (Eph. 2:6). The image of God in us was once under human will, leading us to adopt the image of death. But in Christ, the image of Christ in us is from Him and toward Him, firmly established in Him.

Our original inheritance was to remain in fellowship with God, guaranteed by observing the commandments. However, our new inheritance comes with a new guarantee that is not dependent on our actions. "*The gift of God is without repentance*" (Rom.11:29). This gift of God to us is for eternal salvation, according to Christ's righteousness, power, and faithfulness. As the Apostle says, "*For all the promises of God in Him are Yes, and in Him Amen, to the glory of God through us*" (2 Cor.1:20).

This tremendous transformation occurred through the power of our Lord and according to the measure of grace, not according to human ability. Humanity has advanced toward a new stature — the stature of Christ (Eph.4:13) — which is not merely human but the full and perfect stature that is not subject to corruption, death, or sin. This stature has attained glory and strength through its union with the Son's divinity, a union beyond the measures of the old creation, which has faded with the old covenant of Moses but has been renewed with the new covenant of our Lord Jesus Christ.

The Indwelling of the Holy Spirit and the Promise of Resurrection

We firmly hold to the apostolic teaching that we confess, which encompasses the resurrection from the dead, the triumph of life over death in this present age, and the resurrection of our bodies on the final day. Given that this is the inheritance of all believers, how can we justify viewing physical aspects of life — such as eating, sleeping, and other bodily activities — as barriers to the Holy Spirit's presence? The Apostle warns us against sin that grieves the Holy Spirit: "*Do not grieve the Holy Spirit of God*" (Eph.4:30). His concern goes beyond this admonition, suggesting that he foresaw a time when the grace of God might be overshadowed by human nature. He promptly adds, "*by whom you were sealed for the day of redemption*" (Eph.4:30). How could the Holy Spirit depart from us if we become distracted by worldly concerns, especially when the divine seal is firmly established within us?

The evangelist warns us: "*But you have an anointing from the Holy One, and you know all things. You know the truth, and no lie is of the truth. Who is the liar but he who denies that Jesus is the Christ? This is the antichrist, who denies the Father and the Son*" (1 John. 2:20-22). The truth — Jesus, who became "*Christ the Lord*" — affirms that this anointing is for us, and to deny it is to reject both the giver, the Father, and the recipient, the incarnate Son. Thus, anyone who denies this anointing is a liar and "*is not of the truth*" (1 John. 2:21); they do not possess Christ and are not aligned with Him, as they deny "*the anointing of the*

Holy One" (1 John. 2:20), which is the anointing of Jesus who became the Christ.

The Trinity has placed this seal upon us, confirmed by the prayers of sacred baptism, symbolizing the light we have received. As the Apostle Paul states, we were once "*darkness, but now you are light in the Lord*" (Eph.5:8). Therefore, he warns us: "*Do not participate in the unfruitful works of darkness*" (Eph.5:11), referring to the sinful behaviors that turn us away from the light. However, the hope placed in the Holy Spirit is unshakable and enduring. As the Apostle encourages: "*Awake, you who sleep, arise from the dead, and Christ will give you light*" (Eph.5:14).

The Impact of Sin on the Body and Spirit: Understanding the Dichotomy

According to apostolic teaching, "*the wages of sin is death*" (Rom.6:23). Death introduces a profound sense of disdain towards the body. The body, inherently frail and subject to the inexorable march of aging, inevitably becomes a source of contempt due to its decline over time. However, this disdain rooted in our love for God is markedly different from the contempt resulting from death and aging.

True love for God does not cultivate contempt for the body. Instead, it fosters compassion, tenderness, and unwavering appreciation for all that God has created. This love enables us to remain steadfast in our devotion even when confronted with suffering or illness. We learn to accept all circumstances with gratitude, recognizing that God is active in all situations for the benefit of those who love Him (Rom.8:28). This perspective reframes our view of the body, encouraging us to see it as a divine creation worthy of respect and care.

Conversely, the disdain for the body that arises from death is a consequence of sin. Sin creates an internal conflict, dividing our feelings towards the body. We find ourselves in a paradox where we simultaneously love and despise our physical form because it fails to satisfy the deeper needs and desires of our hearts. This internal discord contributes to a phenomenon known as *"smallness of heart,"* where individuals who lack physical attractiveness, have disabilities, or have experienced loss of body parts may suffer from diminished self-worth and dissatisfaction. Such individuals, like all others, may place undue emphasis on the body's external appearance, overlooking the true, glorified nature revealed through baptism and divine anointing.

Sin engenders a sense of *"revulsion"* and dissatisfaction towards the body. This feeling of revulsion is reminiscent of the shame Adam felt in Genesis when he covered himself after realizing his nakedness. This shame is a remnant of Adam's sin, reflecting a deep-seated discomfort with the body. However, those who have embraced the purity of Christ do not experience such shame. Instead, they view their bodies as a visible manifestation of the spirit — a temporary abode within the original creation. They understand that a greater reality awaits them in the new creation, exemplified by the Lord Jesus Christ, the firstborn from the dead. Christ leads us in all things so that all members may receive the anointing, as highlighted in Psalm 133:3, where it is said, *"There the Lord commanded the blessing,"* symbolizing the unity and sanctity of the church, the body of Christ.

Alienation of the Body from the Spirit

Sin also leads to a fragmented perception of oneself, marking a sign of spiritual death. It distorts our understanding of the body, leading us to believe that it represents the ultimate form of existence and the ultimate goal of life. In our quest for pleasure, the body is treated as if it were a separate entity, rather than an integral part of our true selves. This distortion causes the body to become alienated from the mind, will, and emotions, reducing it to a mere tool for achieving pleasure.

When we perceive our bodies as foreign or alien, it can lead to feelings of *"smallness of heart"* and a sense of life's futility. This experience is not true humility. Genuine humility is not derived from a sense of life's insignificance but from a profound encounter with the love of God. When a person experiences the deep love of their Creator and is enlightened by the humility of the Holy Spirit, true humility becomes a lasting aspect of their inner life. It is akin to a poor person entering the presence of a majestic king and realizing their own poverty in contrast to the king's grandeur. This awareness of one's own limitations remains ever-present as long as the person is alive.

Confessing our sins leads to repentance rather than genuine humility. The act of confession within the church is an acknowledgment that the minister of the sacraments is our High Priest, the Lord Jesus Christ, and that the power at work is the power of the Holy Spirit. This recognition reinforces the understanding that true humility and transformation come not from a sense of inadequacy but from a heartfelt relationship with God, who is the source of all grace and redemption.

The Divine Love for Sinners and the Promise of Renewal

In conclusion, it is crucial to fully grasp that the Lord's love for sinners is boundless and unconditional. This profound truth is continually affirmed every time we address God as *"Lover of mankind"* in our prayers—a name we hold dear because it highlights God's focus on our intrinsic humanity rather than our transgressions. We are reminded that *"No one is pure and without blemish, even if they lived only one day on earth,"* emphasizing the universal need for divine grace and forgiveness.

Every year, as we celebrate the Feast of Pentecost, we publicly acknowledge and declare that the fruits of life, sustained by the Holy Spirit—the Spirit of Life—are evidence of God's redemptive work. This feast is a powerful testament to the restoration of the divine image, which was lost due to Adam's sin. By the grace of God, we have been returned to our original state of dignity and purpose, enabling us to engage in our earthly tasks with renewed joy and vigor. The first curse has been lifted, and although the earth still bears thorns, it now yields its fruits as a blessing because the new life has been interwoven with the old creation.

This transformation continues until the promised day of liberation when *"death will be swallowed up by life"* (2 Cor.5:4).

This renewal extends to our own bodies. We have been spiritually anointed by the Holy Spirit in our *"inner man"* and physically marked through the sacrament of baptism, which consecrates our physical being. Even though we still experience bodily suffering and weakness, this does not diminish the significance of the divine anointing we have received. We look forward to the ultimate freedom from the corruption of the old creation, as the Spirit of Life has instilled in us *"the life of Jesus."* This profound spiritual renewal ensures that we will be resurrected and restored in the full glory of Christ's resurrection. Thus, our daily struggles and weaknesses are met with the assurance that God's transformative power is at work within us, preparing us for the eternal life to come.

Part Two

From Spiritual Death to Eternal Life: Sin, Repentance, Divine Justice, and the Promise of Resurrection

Understanding Sin and Redemption

When exploring the nature of sin, we find that sin, death, and the devil are closely intertwined as a unified force, all stemming from transgression. The Bible teaches us that sin and death are inseparable; sin exists only in those who fall short of God's glory (Rom.3:23), and death is the inevitable result of sin (Rom.6:23). The devil, however, is the ultimate source of temptation and the primary cause of turning away from God's truth and natural order (1 John. 3:8).

Jesus Christ's mission was to abolish both sin and death. By conquering death, He effectively separated it from sin and stripped the devil, who wielded power over death, of his authority (Col.1:15). The Scriptures reveal that sin, along with death and the devil, constitutes the source of darkness, corruption, and moral failure (John.8:12).

To understand the roots of sin, consider the concept of the lust for power. This desire originated with the devil, who sought to exalt himself above God and tempted Adam to do likewise (Is.14:13-14). This temptation led to Adam's spiritual death and, eventually, his physical death. Although Adam did not die immediately after the fall, he lived his life outside of Paradise, marked by the seed of death planted in his spirit (Gen.3:6). In response, God planted the seed of life in the human heart, nurtured by the Spirit of life that raised Jesus from the dead (John 10:10; Rom.8:11).

So, did Jesus die both spiritually and physically on the cross, like Adam? The answer is both yes and no. Jesus took upon Himself the judgment that was due to us (Is.53:5), but He tore up the *certificate* of judgment that stood against us (Col. 2:14). By nailing it to the cross, He removed the barrier of sin and death. This would not have been possible if Jesus had merely experienced a spiritual death like Adam. The apostle Peter affirmed on Pentecost that death could not "*hold*" Him (Acts.2:24), as Jesus overcame it.

The authority of judgment belongs solely to the Triune God—Father, Son, and Holy Spirit (Matt.28:18). The just Judge does not answer to anyone but acts according to His own goodness (Ps.50:6). Just as clay does not question the potter about its shape (Is. 29:16; Rom.9:20-21), God acts according to His divine will. When we affirm that Jesus truly died, we recognize that His soul was separated from His body, akin to Adam's death. Yet, we must also remember that Jesus possesses the authority of life. He descended into hell, not as a victim of death's power, but to defeat the forces of darkness, scatter the powers of hell, break the grip of death, and annul the certificate of judgment (1 Peter. 3:19; Rev.1:18).

In contrast, many people today admire pride and the quest for power, viewing humility as weakness. This perspective reflects a disconnect from the Son of God and mirrors the devil's desire to be like God and overthrow Him (Ezek.28:17). Adam's redemption came through the death and humility of Christ, which the cross alone reveals. The cross is the ultimate measure of true power—defined by love and humility, as demonstrated by Jesus (Phil.2:7-8).

Spiritual Death and Hell: Two Sides of the Same Coin

Spiritual death and hell are deeply intertwined aspects of the same existential reality. Hell is not merely a place of torment but represents a state of existence characterized by stagnation and lack of purpose. It embodies a life disconnected from growth and fulfilment, where potential remains unfulfilled and aspirations are continually thwarted. For humanity, created in the image of God, to live without God is to become a mere shadow of oneself, confined to a limited and stagnant state. This self-imposed confinement prevents individuals from transcending their mere human nature and fully realizing their divine potential.

In this self-imposed state, humanity struggles against the divine image within, leading to an alienation from our true selves and entrapment in a false existence that we have fashioned for ourselves. As Paul writes in Romans 8:3, *"For what the Law was powerless to do because it was weakened by the flesh, God did by sending his own Son in the likeness of sinful flesh to be a sin offering."* Jesus entered into this condition of spiritual death and physical mortality to transform it. His physical death was not just an end but a pathway to overcoming sin and death itself, striving to live in full dependence on God's grace — the ultimate source of true life.

Jesus and the Restoration of Life

Jesus, however, did more than merely experience death; He embraced our human nature and restored it to eternal life through His union with the divine essence of the Trinity — Father, Son, and Holy Spirit. His death on the cross was a decisive act of condemning sin and rejecting a life that does not acknowledge or accept God. Unlike Adam, who fell into sin and remained estranged, Jesus' death put an end to this estrangement and restored the body to unity with God and the inner life.

The body becomes alienated from the human spirit when it becomes an instrument of sin. This alienation results in a perversion of natural life, leading to a state where sin shapes existence and ultimately binds one to death. Paul describes these actions as "*the works of the dead flesh*" in Galatians 5:19: "*The acts of the flesh are obvious: sexual immorality, impurity, and debauchery.*" These actions are devoid of life, leading to separation from ourselves, our bodies, and God—the true source of life.

Is Spiritual Death a Separation from God?

Human existence often diverges from its intended purpose. No being in heaven or on earth possesses life independently; all existence is sustained solely by God's power. God alone is eternal, as expressed in Exodus 3:14, "*I AM WHO I AM.*" Humans are reflections of this divine existence. Separation from God originates solely from our own choices, manifesting as a rejection of His commandments and a pursuit of power devoid of love and humility—mirroring the life of the devil, who sought to be like God without God. Understanding that this separation is from our side is crucial. God has not severed His life from us but has preserved the grace of our existence. As Paul states in Acts 17:28, "*For in him we live and move and have our being,*" and as Revelation 21:5 affirms, "*He who was seated on the throne said, 'I am making everything new!'*"

We must not fall into despair, as God has not abandoned humanity but has continually reached out through prophets, laws, and revelations of righteousness. Even the worship of non-believers reflects an innate search for the Creator, despite the obscuration of understanding, as stated in Romans 1:20: *"For since the creation of the world God's invisible qualities—his eternal power and divine nature—have been clearly seen, being understood from what has been made, so that people are without excuse."*

Signs of Separation from God and Spiritual Death

Several indicators of separation from God and spiritual death include:

1. Ignorance of our Creator, particularly His goodness and love. This ignorance is reflected in 2 Corinthians 4:4: *"The god of this age has blinded the minds of unbelievers, so that they cannot see the light of the gospel that displays the glory of Christ, who is the image of God."*

2. The misconception that one is the source of their own life and that material sustenance is the key to existence. Jesus warned against this in Matthew 6:31-32: *"So do not worry, saying, 'What shall we eat?' or 'What shall we drink?' or 'What shall we wear?' For the pagans run after all these things, and your heavenly Father knows that you need them."* Jesus highlighted God's provision for all creation—lilies and birds alike—to expose the ignorance of God, an early sign of spiritual death. This false sense of immortality breeds pride. If God is

indeed the source of life, why should we be proud? What authority do we have to determine the fates of others?

3. Believing that "*transgression*" leads to a better existence or growth. This misconception is challenged by James 1:14-15: *"But each person is tempted when they are dragged away by their own evil desire and enticed. Then, after desire has conceived, it gives birth to sin; and sin, when it is full-grown, gives birth to death."*

4. Doubting the wisdom of God's commandments, considering them to be weakness, and believing that self-defined goodness surpasses divine goodness. Proverbs 14:12 warns, *"There is a way that appears to be right, but in the end it leads to death."* Choosing good and evil based on personal desires and pride is essentially *"transgression."* In summary, spiritual death equates to hell, and hell represents a life constrained by fragmented goals, devoid of growth, vision, or experience beyond the physical and these disjointed aims that fragment human existence.

An Example of Spiritual Death on Earth

Consider an individual consumed by hatred and enmity, making an enemy the centre of their existence. This enmity becomes all-encompassing, defining their entire being. As they seek to escape this torment, they often find themselves sinking deeper into anger. Ironically, the quest for freedom is thwarted by pride, which pulls them back into hatred. This scenario represents a temporal, miniature version of spiritual death or a "*small hell*," which the Lord does not abandon but approaches. As Jesus illustrates in Matthew 18:34-35: "*In anger his master handed him over to the jailers to be tortured, until he should pay back all he owed. This is how my heavenly Father will treat each of you unless you forgive your brother or sister from your heart.*" Thus, we can say that hell is not just a distant realm but can be present in the heart of the individual.

The Authority of Satan and Genuine Repentance

God, our Creator, did not grant Satan any authority over us or even over irrational creatures. When Satan requested permission to enter the pigs, their subsequent destruction symbolized the end of Satan's dominion. Even righteous Job was tested in every way, but God did not allow the tempter to control Job's mind. So how did Satan gain power over death?

Temptation initially brought humanity and Satan together. After Satan's fall from grace, he sought to bring humanity down, knowing that humans were destined to inherit the promise. Thus, temptation ensnares both unwary humans and Satan, including the wise who rely on worldly wisdom. When they fall, they join forces with Satan, who becomes the centre of temptation. Despite this, the human heart, mired in sin, remains beyond the enemy's direct control. Satan can only "*guess*" at our inner struggles by observing our outward reactions and behaviours, which reveal the state of our inner selves. Temptation, therefore, acts as bait, used by the enemy to capture us.

Indicators of Genuine Repentance

True repentance involves a deep connection with the Lord, seeking guidance from the Scriptures and spiritual mentors, and heeding the Holy Spirit's voice in our hearts. It requires prioritizing God's commandments over worldly wisdom.

Love must govern every thought, word, and action. This is reflected in our readiness to forgive offenses and respond to insults with the spirit of Jesus, as He instructs in Matthew 5:44: *"But I tell you, love your enemies and pray for those who persecute you."*

Genuine repentance also means staying faithful to Jesus' teachings, even during periods of doubt. Crying out for God's grace and strength is a sign of repentance, as stated in 2 Corinthians 12:9: *"But he said to me, 'My grace is sufficient for you, for my power is made perfect in weakness.'"*

We must prioritize the cross and the crucified Christ above everything, even life itself. Paul underscores this in Philippians 3:8: *"What is more, I consider everything a loss because of the surpassing worth of knowing Christ Jesus my Lord, for whose sake I have lost all things. I consider them garbage, that I may gain Christ."*

Additionally, we must develop a profound hatred for sin coupled with humility towards sinners. Hatred for sin without humility risks becoming a defence of our own reputation and seeking hidden praise. True humility involves recognizing our own need for grace, as exemplified by Jesus' words in John 8:7: *"Let any one of you who is without sin be the first to throw a stone at her."*

The Meaning of Christ's Wounds and the Hope of Resurrection

When Jesus rose from the dead as the "*first fruits of those who have fallen asleep*" (1 Cor.15:20), He chose to retain the wounds of the cross — the nail marks in His hands and feet and the spear wound in His side. Thomas the Apostle, upon seeing these marks, declared, "*My Lord and my God*" (John.20:28). Although Jesus' resurrection restored His body to an incorruptible state, He preserved these wounds as an everlasting testament to His boundless love for humanity. These wounds reveal three profound and interconnected truths:

First, before His crucifixion, Jesus revealed His divine glory on Mount Tabor during the Transfiguration. He allowed Peter, James, and John to witness His divine radiance, which had been veiled in His human form. This event was a glimpse of the divine glory that will be fully revealed to us at the resurrection. As Jesus prayed in John 17:22, "*I have given them the glory that you gave me, that they may be one as we are one.*" This divine light, which shone through Him on Mount Tabor, is a promise of the transformed state our bodies will attain on the final day. This transformation is not merely a future hope but a present reality that is sometimes visible in the lives of saints, whose holiness reflects the divine light they have embraced.

Second, the retention of the cross's wounds by Jesus is a profound affirmation of His love for humanity. These wounds are not merely marks of His suffering but symbols of His transformative love. By retaining these wounds, Jesus demonstrates that love can sanctify and elevate our physical existence. The nails that pierced His hands and feet and the crown of thorns He wore are visible manifestations of His love's power. They reveal that true love, rooted in sacrifice, has the power to transform our very being. Jesus accepted the nails in His hands and feet, symbolizing the visible and transformative power of His love and how it sanctifies and elevates the body. The crown of thorns, which caused Him physical pain, also represents His triumph over sin and His cleansing of our spiritual wounds. The spear wound in His side, from which flowed blood and water, symbolizes the birth of the Church, representing spiritual birth and the outpouring of grace. Reflecting on these wounds, we are reminded that, even while living in our *"body of death"* (Rom.7:24), we experience the signs of resurrection. As Paul explains in 1 Corinthians 15:42-44, our natural bodies, though perishable and weak, will be transformed into bodies of glory, power, and immortality.

Third, the incarnation, death, and resurrection of Jesus reveal the profound mystery of the union between the soul and the body. Jesus came to redeem us, embracing us as a shepherd embraces his flock. This embrace illustrates that the soul is the essence of human existence, while the body is its external form. Through His incarnation, Jesus renewed the soul and restored it to its heavenly image, as foretold in the Gospel. This renewal begins with spiritual transformation and will be completed at the resurrection. Baptism symbolizes this renewal, cleansing the body from the curse of death and anticipating the resurrection to eternal life. The indwelling of the Holy Spirit in both soul and body sanctifies the body in baptism, ensuring its preservation despite physical decay. The departed saints, who lived out their faith and followed Christ, are honoured as holy beings. They serve as living testimonies to the transformative power of Christ's love. Their bodies, even in death, remain temples of the Holy Spirit, who dwells within them. Everything is sealed by the Holy Spirit, reflecting the glorious image of Jesus. We eagerly await the day when Christ will transform our humble bodies to be like His glorious body (Phil.3:21). This transformation is not only a future promise but a present hope that invites us to experience the fullness of the Lord's goodness and grace, embracing the healing and renewal of our entire being through union with Him in the mystery of His sacrificial love.

In contemplating the significance of Christ's wounds, we are invited to understand the deep connection between His suffering and our spiritual renewal. The wounds bear witness to His love and His victory over death, while offering us a tangible assurance of the resurrection and the transformation that awaits us. Through His wounds, we are reminded of the profound truth that our own transformation is already underway, and we live in hopeful anticipation of the day when all things will be made new in Christ.

Triumph Over Death and the Mystery of Final Renewal

The Lord's victory over Satan is profound and multifaceted. By expelling Satan and imprisoning him in hell, Jesus decisively crushed the power of evil. On the cross, He confronted and defeated death itself, declaring forgiveness to those who sought it while suffering in agony. His sacrifice was not in vain; it transformed the very nature of death and opened up the possibilities of redemption. Through His suffering, Jesus brought about a series of miraculous events: He opened paradise to the repentant thief, raised the dead, restored sight to the blind, and healed the sick. These acts were not mere displays of power but affirmations of His divine authority and a promise of a future resurrection and renewal.

In light of these extraordinary achievements, it is perplexing to consider why remnants of sin still persist. If Jesus has eradicated all sin and restored us to a divine, heavenly existence through spiritual rebirth, why do we continue to witness decay and return to dust? The Apostle Paul addresses this dilemma in Romans 8:21, where he clearly states that the complete renewal of creation will be accomplished on the final day. Although we have been redeemed in our inner selves, we still "*groan inwardly as we wait eagerly for our adoption to sonship, the redemption of our bodies*" (Rom.8:23). This physical renewal will only happen in conjunction with the rest of creation.

We currently live in a state where our bodies face death because the cosmic order has not yet been fully restored. We are still waiting for the "*revelation of the glorious freedom of the children of God*" (Rom.8:21). This waiting period is a crucial aspect of our faith journey. It is a time of anticipation and patience as we await the Lord's return, which will restore the cosmic order and complete the renewal of all creation.

How Did the Lord Remove the Curse of Death, and Why Do We Still Die and Are Buried?

Understanding the term "*curse*" is key to grasping this concept. In biblical terms, a curse is something that God refuses to sustain or enhance. It is a condition of decline and barrenness. The resurrection of Jesus, who took on human flesh from the Virgin Mary and was glorified through the resurrection, signifies that the curse has been completely abolished. If the curse of death were still in effect, resurrection would be impossible.

Jesus transformed death, which was the result of sin, into a force that now contributes to the renewal of creation. Death's former power of decay and dissolution has been converted into a mechanism that facilitates the birth of new life. The passing away of the old creation signifies the birth of the new. As such, Christians experience death differently from non-believers. For us, death is not a final end but a transformation that leads to salvation. Our death is in the Lord, and our rest is in Him. This perspective means that our death is considered a form of salvation, whereas the death of the wicked results in judgment.

Christians undergo death once, symbolically crucified and buried with Christ. The Apostle Paul emphasizes that it is not Christ who is buried with us but that we are *buried with Him and in Him.* This distinction highlights that Jesus took on our nature, but He is also the first fruits of those who have fallen asleep. We are buried with Him because He has abolished the power of the grave.

Our approach to death should be characterized by faith and hope rather than despair. We should not mourn the dead like those without hope. Our mourning is tinged with faith, believing that the departed are with the Lord. While we grieve the loss of our loved ones, we find comfort in the belief that they are in His presence. Thus, we die and are buried with the Lord, but His life remains in us. On the cross, He was the living dead, and in the tomb, He rested to defeat the powers of hell. Jesus entered hell with His human nature, united with His divine nature, to destroy hell's power and free the captives, opening the gates of paradise.

There is a significant difference between Jesus being in hell by His divine power and being there with His human nature. His divine power as Creator was never in question. What inspires our praise and honour is

His presence with human nature, united with His divine person. This presence is the source of our faith and hope. He left no place untouched by His salvation—whether in heaven, on earth, or in hell. His descent into hell was not merely an act of power but a profound demonstration of His commitment to deliverance and renewal. He descended to grant believers the power to triumph over death, closing *"the mouth of hell"* forever.

This power of triumph is imparted to all who have received the sacrament of baptism. We are *"buried with Him"* in baptism, and through His victory over hell, Christ has given us the strength to bring *"every thought into captivity to Christ"* (2 Cor.10:5) and to transform every force of evil into a means of grace. His death and resurrection secure our spiritual victory and empower us to live in the light of His promises.

Why Does Renewal Await the Final Day?

As previously mentioned, the process of renewal continues to unfold through death until the final resurrection. This final day will reveal everything that has been *"hidden"* from our eyes. Although this reality is present with us, it remains unseen except through faith—an inner vision awaiting the day appointed by the Lord for the complete renewal of all things. This day will mark the culmination of God's divine plan, the final stage of His providence, and the ultimate restoration of creation.

Understanding the Path to Redemption: The Role of Discipline, Grace, and Spiritual Growth

Returning to a particular sin often signifies a weakness in our love for God. This weakness is not effectively addressed through mere punishment or discipline alone, as such approaches can sometimes lead to feelings of *"low self-esteem"* or *"self-deprecation."* Instead, what we truly need is the transformative love and wisdom of Christ. The Bible describes Christ as someone who *"will not break a bruised reed or quench a smoldering wick,"* a compassionate teacher who searches for the lost sheep, leaving the ninety-nine to find the one who is astray. This gentle approach highlights a core aspect of Christ's character: His dedication to nurturing and guiding the broken rather than condemning them.

Those who lack this understanding should not be entrusted with the responsibility of helping others in need of spiritual guidance. When we talk about *"serving sinners,"* it encompasses everyone, including myself and the entire Church community. We are all sinners; no one is categorically better or worse than another. We are all *"unworthy servants,"* often driven by fear of punishment and desire for reward in our attempts to repent. This approach can make our repentance fall short of true love's fire. However, the good and merciful God accepts even this imperfect repentance, showing His boundless grace.

Discipline can be beneficial for those with high aspirations and strong spiritual goals. However, for those overwhelmed by despair and fear, who have fallen into a state of *"self-deprecation,"* harsh discipline may be spiritually detrimental. It can lead to slow spiritual decay if applied without understanding. True discipline should be a healing remedy, not a tool for further suffering. It should motivate the humble-hearted to seek salvation from God. In contrast, those who have repeatedly fallen without genuine repentance may find their diminished humility leading them toward disobedience and rebellion.

It is essential to differentiate between discipline and punishment. Discipline is meant to heal and support those who need it, while punishment often only inflicts additional pain and exacerbates the individual's struggles. Discipline should not be about seeking temporary gains or imposing restrictions; instead, it should aim to teach humility and foster love for others, reducing tendencies toward judgment and condemnation. For individuals prone to anger, practical actions rather than harsh reprimands can serve as discipline. These actions are intended not to punish but to offer constructive support and guidance, helping those with specific weaknesses become valuable members of the community.

The ultimate goal is to reinforce love and maintain the service of others while preserving their dignity. Undermining the dignity of those who fall only deepens their despair, leads to disobedience, and causes them to lose sight of their purpose. In Christ, we are honoured with son-ship and treated by the Heavenly Father as His children. This honour was bestowed even when the apostles, despite witnessing miracles and the Transfiguration, faltered in their faith. Peter, for instance, denied Jesus, and others fled during His arrest. Despite these failings, Jesus did not rebuke them harshly. Instead, He gently addressed Thomas, saying, "*Because you have seen me, you have believed*" (John. 20:29), reminding him of the miracles he had witnessed and extending grace and reassurance.

We should strive to emulate Christ's gentleness and patience, offering healing rather than harshness. Spiritual guidance should be grounded in gospel wisdom, treating each sinner as an equal heir in the kingdom and as a beloved child of the Father. For individuals repeatedly falling into a specific sin, they may not need strict discipline but rather comfort and strong teaching about God's unwavering love. This love can restore their dignity and remind them of their worth. Self-contempt can lead to repeated failures, and failing to recognize one's dignity as a child of God can perpetuate these issues. Addressing such conditions requires a blend of prayer, teaching, and reflection on heavenly matters and the life of Jesus Christ. This approach strengthens fellowship with the Lord and provides solace.

Ultimately, recurring sins are best addressed with gospel wisdom that preserves the sinner's dignity, encourages engagement with scripture, and fosters excellence in service. These measures help restore their dignity and promote self-reflection, supporting their spiritual growth. This holistic approach aligns with the broader grace of God, allowing us to navigate the complexities of this world with peace, tranquillity, and renewed purpose.

Understanding the Grace of Baptism and the Nature of Sin

Baptism is regarded as an *"indelible seal,"* which is why it is given only once. This sacrament signifies our rebirth through the Father by His Son, Jesus Christ, and by the grace of the Holy Spirit. For this reason, we do not re-baptize those who have fallen away but rather welcome their repentance. Baptism is never repeated for those who have received it within the universal Church. As the Apostle Paul explains, grace is fundamentally different from sin, and the gift of grace cannot be compared to the fall. The contrast between the first Adam and the last Adam, Jesus Christ, is significant. The Apostle encapsulates this teaching by stating, "*The gifts and calling of God are irrevocable*" (Rom.11:29), meaning that Jesus does not regret the gifts He has given us, including forgiveness, the promise of the kingdom, and the indwelling of the Holy Spirit.

When a person returns to their previous sinful state, their past sins are not counted against them. As Paul assures us, our previous sins are not held against us (Rom.14:12; 2 Cor.5:10). The core teaching of the Apostles is succinctly expressed as, "*According to Your mercy, O Lord, and not according to our sins.*" This means that when a person repents, their past sins are forgiven and erased by the grace of God. Paul notes that God does not hold the past sins of the Gentiles against them (Rom.3:25), emphasizing that the gospel of grace and salvation is given freely.

Those approaching baptism do so not as saints but as sinners seeking forgiveness. The Lord does not count our forgiven sins against us. Judgment is not based on the quantity of sins but on the quality of our love and actions. Thus, judgment is summarized in the phrase "*according to their deeds,*" reflecting the ultimate goals we pursued and the service we offered to the Lord and to others. Acts of love are meant to achieve one goal: love itself. As the Lord says, "*I was hungry, and you gave Me food; I was thirsty, and you gave Me drink; I was a stranger, and you took Me in*" (Matt.25:35-36). He identifies with those in need because they are His brothers through His incarnation.

Disregarding the dignity of son-ship is comparable to Esau's sin of trading his birth right for a meal of lentils, which the Apostle describes as "*profane*" (Heb.12:16). Blurring the distinctions between good and evil, sacred and profane, heavenly and earthly destroys our inner life and diminishes our understanding of human dignity. Consider the case of someone living in a royal palace but ending up eating with pigs, like the prodigal son who squandered his inheritance. When he returns, his father restores his former honour. If someone does not return to their original love, warnings and threats may not help; instead, they might lead to hypocrisy and concealment of their sins.

A person who is "*profane*" fails to grasp or appreciate heavenly things or the difference between the Creator and the created. They do not recognize the difference between natural longings and those inspired by the Holy Spirit. Natural longings are the created nature's thirst for its Creator, while the Holy Spirit's inspiration represents the Creator's profound love for the created. This divine love led God to become incarnate and live among us. Faith leads to love, and love nurtures faith. Faith, illuminated by the Holy Spirit, grows in knowledge and produces fruit. Knowledge liberates the will and heart from ignorance. The gift of new life comes from God, who grants us the life of His Son and anoints us so we may inherit the imperishable kingdom with Him.

Those who are "*profane*" need a trained spiritual guide to illuminate their path with teaching, open the door to eternal life, and lead them to the wellspring of living water, the Holy Spirit.

Understanding the Concept of Hell in Christian Theology

What about the concept of hell? It's essential to understand that in Christian belief, Christ triumphed over hell and nullified its power through His death on the cross. Unlike the common interpretation of biblical descriptions of heaven above, the earth below, and the abyss beneath as referring to a dark, subterranean pit where souls are imprisoned, the Bible does not depict hell as a place created by God to confine human souls. Instead, terms like "*the grave*" and "*the abyss*" are used to describe a state of existence outside the divine order established by God—a sort of spiritual wasteland or repository for what is not essential to God's creation.

There is no explicit mention in the Book of Genesis or other scriptures suggesting that God created hell as a realm for punishing human souls. Rather, "*the grave*" *and* "*the abyss*" represent a condition of being outside the ordered universe that God designed. This state can be compared to a collection point for what has no place within God's creation, akin to a landfill created by humans to manage waste. This concept is not part of the original divine creation but a human construct in response to the challenges of life.

The idea of hell is not explicitly defined as a divine creation in the holy texts. According to the universal Church's teaching, Christ descended into hell during His crucifixion to liberate those imprisoned by death's curse and to lead them to paradise. Paradise, as described by Jesus when He promised the thief on the cross, "*Today you will be with Me in paradise,*" signifies a state of eternal rest and peace rather than a physical place. This promise illustrates that Jesus would overcome death and offer comfort and peace to the soul of the thief, moving beyond earthly constraints.

Heaven, as depicted in the Gospels, is not a physical location above us but a realm that transcends our material reality. It is described as existing beyond the physical dimensions we perceive, aligning with Jesus' statement about being "*born from above*" (John. 3:33), which signifies a divine origin rather than a physical altitude.

To help people understand these concepts accurately, it is crucial to transition their perceptions from materialistic views to spiritual realities. Misconceptions about the nature of hell and paradise can disrupt spiritual peace, so education must guide individuals from physical interpretations to a higher spiritual understanding.

We reject the notion that God created a place of eternal torment specifically for humans, as there is no scriptural support for such a belief. This idea does not align with the divine goodness and justice depicted in the Bible. Imagery of torment in Revelation, such as the lake of fire (Rev.20:19), should be understood symbolically. It represents a state of separation from God rather than a literal, physical place of suffering.

References to "*Gehenna*" in the Gospels reflect the corruption of the human heart, which, through sin and separation from God, darkens spiritual understanding. However, God's nature remains untainted by human sin. Those illuminated by the Gospel will see God's true nature and be transformed into His glorious image (1 John.3:2). The vision of the righteous, enlightened by love, contrasts sharply with the vision of the wicked, shrouded in sin.

The details of how the wicked will be excluded from the new heaven and new earth remain unknown, as this future reality has not yet been realized. This aspect of Christian doctrine remains a matter of divine promise through Jesus Christ. For now, it is crucial to maintain our faith, live in holiness while bearing the cross of Christ, and seek the guidance of the Holy Spirit to enlighten our understanding and reveal our inner selves to seasoned spiritual leaders who are well-versed in the teachings of the Gospel.

Understanding Divine Justice

This brings us to a profound exploration of God's justice. It is essential to ask: Is there a distinction between how God teaches about His justice and how non-believers understand it? The answer is undoubtedly yes. Our belief is not confined to the notion of a single deity who merely created the heavens and the earth. We also hold the profound conviction that God sent His only Son into the world for our redemption. Thus, God is both Creator and Redeemer, embodying the one, holy Trinity—one in essence and three in persons. This understanding might seem like an attempt to sidestep the question, but it actually reveals a deeper truth. Belief in the Trinity illuminates our understanding of God's justice in a way that belief in a singular, abstract deity often fails to do. For those who only believe in one God without recognizing the triune nature, the concepts of divine justice, mercy, and love can become muddled and problematic.

Our approach is not to analyse God's attributes separately and then apply these attributes to the Trinity. Nor do we begin with human logic and gradually progress to the divine mysteries of the Trinity. Such a method often leads to errors, which can only be corrected by returning to faith. According to the Apostolic Tradition, as articulated by the Church Fathers, several key truths emerge: Firstly, the Persons of the Trinity—Father, Son, and Holy Spirit—are not separate entities added to God's essence. Rather, they are distinct expressions of the one divine essence. This essence is not merely a collection of attributes but is the divine nature that transcends all human definitions. It represents the singular divine life that exists within the Father, from whom the Son is eternally begotten, and from whom the Holy Spirit proceeds. Therefore, what belongs to the Father is also true of the Son and the Holy Spirit. Consequently, attributes such as love, holiness, power, and justice are inherent to all three Persons of the Trinity. Secondly, everything within God's essence is personified; thus, divine attributes are not impersonal characteristics added to the Father, Son, or Holy Spirit. Love, for instance, is the love of the Father, the Son, and the Holy Spirit. When we hear that "*God is love,*" it refers to the love of the Trinity as a whole. Similarly, when scripture speaks of God's righteousness and justice, it reflects the righteousness and justice of the Father, the Son, and the Holy Spirit—one Trinity in essence, and one essence within the Trinity.

So, what does divine justice entail according to the Church's teaching on the Trinity? It is fundamentally different from the justice practiced by earthly kings, judges, or legal systems. Divine justice is about rewarding according to love and considering the estrangement of humanity from itself and from divine love. This concept is far more nuanced and profound than the justice defined by non-believers, who often rely on legal systems similar to those of ancient civilizations or the Roman Empire. For them, every sin is met with a specific punishment, typically hellfire. This defines their understanding of justice. In contrast, for us, divine justice addresses the human condition in the context of being created in the image and likeness of God, renewed in Christ, and sanctified by the Holy Spirit. It questions what humans have done with their inherent nature and how they have lived as reflections of God's image. This perspective places the justice of the Gospel on a plane that is fundamentally different from that of non-believers.

Why is divine reward based on love?

First and foremost, God's love for sinners is clearly evident in the message of life. The Apostle succinctly captured this divine love: *"For God so loved the world that He gave His only Son"* (John 3:16). This love surpasses all visible and invisible forms of love known to humanity. How could God then reward according to earthly laws that do not fully reveal His love? Instead, according to the love of God revealed in the Son, divine justice is understood as the justice of the one Trinity—the justice of the Saviour who died for us, resurrected us, and granted us the inheritance of the Kingdom. This understanding shifts the focus of judgment from adherence to the law to fellowship with God, and rewards are based not on human achievements or virtues but on faith and spiritual growth in Jesus Christ, the Lord of sinners and the Physician of the fallen.

Second, estrangement from God is preceded by estrangement from oneself and from one's true being—an estrangement that sin exacerbates. For instance, a person who kills learns to destroy life. Scripture states, *"Anyone who hates his brother is a murderer"* (1 John. 3:15), referring not only to physical murder but to the unseen weapon of hatred, which the law cannot address but the Gospel reveals, focusing on the condition of the heart. When a person becomes estranged from their essence, this estrangement cannot be judged merely by the law but must be considered in light of their participation in divine life and the type of corruption that has affected their being. This represents a *"harder judgment"* because the Lord Jesus Christ died for sinners, and judgment is based on life rather than the strict letter of the law.

So If the justice of the Father is the justice of the Son and the Holy Spirit, then is it the justice of the

Father's love, the Son's love, and the Holy Spirit's love? It is challenging to conceptualize the justice of love, whereas separating justice from love is more straightforward. However, this simplistic view does not align with faith. No Person of the Trinity has an attribute that does not exist in the other Persons. Thus, we must ask: What is the justice of love?

First, repaying evil with evil is not a commandment of the Gospel. The one who said, "*You have heard that it was said, 'An eye for an eye'*" (Matt.5:38) contradicted the Jewish legal scholars. The Lord's Prayer, which includes the petition "*And forgive us our debts*" (Matt.6:12), shows that divine justice is not akin to legal justice or the justice of earthly judges.

Second, the law allowed an unintentional killer to seek refuge in "*cities of refuge*" because he did not kill out of malice or hatred. Although he took a life, the law permitted him to live and granted him asylum. If the law, which surpasses the justice of nations, provides the killer a chance at life, then what about the "*second mile*" law, a fragment of God's goodness and patience (Rom. 4:2), which leads us to repentance? What then is the justice of love? What is the justice of the one who sent His only Son? What is the justice of the one who died on the cross? What is the justice of the Holy Spirit who dwells in us? These are the profound questions we must address with the grace we receive from above because the justice of the one who sent His Son—the Father's justice—is to bring us back from the realm of death and its shadows, as "*the light has dawned upon us*" (Matt.4:16). The justice of the one who died for us is to grant paradise to the thief on the cross and to forgive His crucifiers.

The justice of the Holy Spirit is to intercede for us with groans that cannot be expressed in words (Rom.8:26) and to endure the coldness of our hearts, as the Apostle warns: *"Do not quench the Spirit"* (1 Thess.5:19). Thus, we see that the justice of love transcends all known forms of justice.

Therefore, we should not define or limit God's attributes outside the context of the salvation plan revealed in the scriptures and according to the teachings of the holy Fathers. We must speak about God truthfully. When we frame the justice of the Trinity within the context of divine providence, it becomes evident that it is not only the justice of the Trinity's love but also the justice of God's holiness, goodness, and mercy towards humanity. It is a justice that aligns with God's will and is not constrained by external standards. Since the Trinity is not an addition to the essence but one essence and one life, we must recognize that God does not have a nature that imposes constraints or dictates behaviour upon Him, as this is a human concept. Nature and Person together form one reality. We are born with a nature we cannot change but can elevate within certain limits, which does not apply to God. Therefore, it is incorrect to assume that there is a nature opposing a Person or imposing specific behaviours or actions upon Him.

The Divine Mystery of the Son's Self-Emptying

So, who determined that the only Son, the Lord of Glory, should humble Himself and take on the form of a servant? Was it justice, goodness, or love? This question reveals a common pitfall: attempting to dissect God's attributes through a purely human lens, which leads us to a shallow understanding that lacks the depth and nuance of divine mystery. The Son voluntarily chose, out of profound and selfless love for the Father, to assume the form of a servant and take on what is contrary to His divine nature — the finite human nature. But does this mean that the Son became limited by the human body? Absolutely not.

The concept of self-emptying, or "*kenosis*," is not about the Son losing His divine nature or becoming less than God. Instead, it involves the Son voluntarily limiting Himself in terms of experience and function to fully enter into the human condition. This self-emptying was a choice made out of love and obedience, not a transformation of His divine essence. The Son remained fully divine even as He took on human limitations, and He did so with complete freedom and will. His actions were not forced but were carried out according to His own divine plan.

Understanding the nature of this divine self-emptying requires us to move beyond simplistic explanations and embrace the profound depths of the divine plan. The Son's life as a servant, His ascent to Mount Tabor, His power to raise the dead, and His suffering on the cross — all these events are far more than historical occurrences. They represent the complex interplay of divine justice, love, and self-emptying in a way that surpasses human comprehension.

Consider the Son's journey: He, who assumed the role of a servant, also transcended this role by performing acts that are beyond human capability. He climbed Mount Tabor, a symbol of divine revelation, and brought the dead back to life from the farthest reaches of the universe. He endured His own crucifixion, and His soul was suspended in a fiery love that shook the very foundations of creation. These are not mere events to be analysed philosophically; they are profound mysteries to be understood through the lens of divine providence.

The principles of this divine providence are revealed in several key ways:

1. *Divine Purpose for Our Benefit*: Everything the Lord did was for our advancement and well-being. His actions were driven by a purpose that transcends mere justice or love, aiming at our ultimate good.

2. *Unchanging Divine Nature*: Even in His self-emptying, the Son remained the singular Lord and incarnate God. He did not oscillate between being God and being human; rather, He maintained an inseparable union of divinity and humanity. This unity is essential and cannot be divided or altered.

3. *Victory Over Death*: In His death, which paradoxically gives life, the Son experienced death in His flesh to destroy it from within. He allowed death to confront Him so that He could obliterate it. This act was a profound defeat of death itself, showing His mastery over it.

4. *Triumphant Over Hell*: The Son conquered Hell with the power of His divine nature, using His human experience to pierce through the darkness of Hell like lightning, dismantling all forces of darkness. This demonstrates that His triumph was not merely a display of power but a profound act of divine justice and love.

The Lord did not act out of mere justice or love in isolation but with a form of justice that encompasses and transcends human understanding. This justice is deeply intertwined with the divine mystery of self-emptying, which is beyond any conventional interpretation of justice or love. To fully grasp the implications of this divine act, we must recognize that God's nature and actions cannot be confined to human categories but must be understood within the broader framework of divine providence and the ineffable mystery of the Trinity.

Understanding the Nature of Evil and Its Resolution in Christ

In exploring the concept of evil and its nature, it is crucial to understand that evil does not exist as a distinct creation by God. The apostle's statement, "*He Himself bore our sins in His body on the tree*," raises an important question: If God did not create evil, how is it that Jesus bore our sins?

All created natures receive their existence, life, and purpose from God, who brought everything into being through His Son, Jesus Christ. Therefore, evil was not created by God and does not have a nature of its own. Instead, it emerges from human choices — our thoughts, will, relationships, and how we interact with creation. Evil arises from humanity's misuse of freedom and creation. Since God is inherently good, evil does not originate from Him; rather, it stems from humanity's misuse of freedom and creation.

Evil, much like its creators — the devil and humans — lacks the capacity to endure. It is not a substance created from nothing like the creation of God; instead, it is a concept that exists only in the minds of its creators. God created iron, for instance, but did not instruct humanity to make weapons of war from it. The prophet Isaiah foretells that these instruments of war will eventually be destroyed and transformed into tools for harvesting (Isaiah 2:4). Thus, what was created will eventually decay or lose its intended purpose due to God's goodness, making the eternal existence of evil impossible. Naturally, we are horrified by evils such as murder and torture — things that deeply distress the human heart and leave wounds that take time to heal.

When considering how the Lord bore our sins in His body on the cross, according to the apostolic faith, we recognize that our actions do not last; they are fleeting like smoke or grass. When the Saviour came to the *"birth pangs"* of salvation and the renewal of humanity, He transformed the old humanity through His birth from the Virgin Mary by the Holy Spirit, His anointing in the Jordan, and His trials in the wilderness. He then went to Golgotha to offer Himself as a sin offering for us. This offering involved the entire Trinity and humanity — He offered Himself to the Father, His divine Person, and the Holy Spirit. It was a singular offering by a singular priest for the one Trinity. The Son shares the same life as the Father and the Holy Spirit, and thus He could not present the offering without it being acceptable to the same offering because He possesses the same honour, glory, and power as the Father and the Holy Spirit. This means that everything He did for us originated from Him, existed through Him, and was offered by Him, and it is as much His as it is the Father's and the Holy Spirit's. Thus, the offering of Himself as a sacrifice is also His own.

When our Lord Jesus Christ willingly accepted His suffering, the burden of human sins was not a physical load but was inherent in the human nature He bore. The sins of past and future times — those before His life-giving death and those to come after His death and resurrection — were essentially embedded in human nature. The Lord returned to the source, the human heart that does not know its Creator. At this source, He encountered hatred and enmity towards God, fellow humans, and all creation.

He also found the dominance of lust, injustice, and other evils that originate from a false divinity invented by humanity. As the Psalm says, "*I said, 'You are gods,' but you will die like mere mortals*" (Ps.82:6). This false divinity was crucified on the cross. In profound humility and deep anguish, He cried out to the Father, "*My God, My God, why have You forsaken Me?*" (Ps.22:1), acknowledging that the false divinity clashes with the true, incarnate God. The devil had told humanity, "*You will be like God*" (Gen.3:5). However, humanity did not become like God but rather like its fallen self, returning to nothingness from which it was created, devoid of true purpose and the image of God.

The Saviour experienced this emptiness, which stemmed from the original nature created from nothing and dependent on God for existence. Thus, the Lord cried out in profound pain because the true God from the true God, Light from Light, took the place of all rebels and deniers. This was not merely a quantitative burden but a qualitative one — humanity's descent into pride and false existence, existence without God. As the Psalm says, "*The fool says in his heart, 'There is no God'*" (Ps.14:1). This godless existence is humanity's reality, the existence that was crucified on the cross and cried out, "*Why have You forsaken Me?*" because it found darkness and death. Yet, when death collided with life, life triumphed, and the new humanity emerged victorious. Thus, the glory of this victory belongs to Him forever and ever.

The Return to the Self:
A Path to Spiritual Rebirth

Our Lord, in His divine wisdom, describes the *"prodigal son"* as one who *"came to himself"* (Luke. 15:17). This profound moment of self-realization marks the beginning of a spiritual journey back to God. The act of *"returning"* or *"repentance"* signifies more than a mere change of mind; it represents the initial step towards reuniting with God, whose nature is transcendent and distinct from anything created.

To truly embrace faith, we must first learn to love ourselves authentically. Genuine self-love is not merely a sentiment but a foundational principle that guides us towards choosing faith, recognizing its inherent goodness and righteousness.

The process of spiritual awakening starts with the return to oneself. This involves recognizing and confronting the illusions and false deities that reside within us. False deities, in this sense, are the human-made constructs where individuals create their own moral standards apart from God. This separation leads to a distorted understanding of good and evil and ultimately results in spiritual death.

How did evil bring about both spiritual and physical death? The answer lies in humanity's fall from its original state. Originally created in the image of God, humanity was endowed with existence, freedom, and life derived from God. However, through the fall, humanity transformed from a being reflecting God's image — whose existence and freedom were sustained by God — to a being defined solely by human nature, which was created from nothing and lacks an inherent source of life. As the divine life drained away, humanity experienced spiritual death. Only the grace of God preserved humanity from a complete return to nothingness.

But, Why did God permit humanity's transgression? The first reason is that freedom of choice is essential for true love. Love cannot be coerced; it must be freely given and received. Coercion only breeds rebellion. Thus, when humanity exercised its freedom to choose self-love apart from God, it fell into disobedience. The second reason is that true fellowship requires love, and love necessitates freedom of choice. By transgressing, humanity rejected divine fellowship and sought life within itself. Unable to find it, death—the fear of death— entered the human consciousness, deepening the transgression.

Regarding how Adam and Eve could procreate after the fall, it is crucial to understand that God had already promised a blessing before the fall: "*Be fruitful and multiply*" (Gen.1:28). Even after the fall, God did not retract His promise. As a partner in humanity's journey, God accepted the fall but ensured that humanity would not return to nothingness. His love for humanity remained steadfast, and He prepared for redemption through the cross.

The return to oneself is essentially a rediscovery of the "*original state*," or the image of God. Sin represents a departure from this divine image and an immersion in a self-created existence devoid of God. This existence may seem alive but cannot sustain itself eternally. "*Death is the separation of the soul from God*"—a separation resulting from our choices and a fall into a self-empty existence. The Saviour articulated this when He said, "*Whoever finds their life will lose it*" (Matt.10:39). Those who find themselves apart from God confine their existence within themselves. Conversely, "*whoever loses their life for My sake will find it*" (Matt.10:39), indicating that self-sacrifice leads to true life. Since sacrifice involves fellowship, He added, "*for My sake and for the gospel*" (Mark 8:35). He also questioned, "*What good is it for someone to gain the whole world, yet forfeit their soul?*" (Mark. 8:36). What appears as gain often costs one's essence, enslaving one to possessions. Death introduces excessive attachment to material things and fosters selfishness. Those who accumulate wealth live not only for themselves. When they share with others, they fear losing possessions, despite our Lord's clear command. He illustrated the folly of the rich man who lost everything because his life was taken, saying, "*This is how it will be with whoever stores up things for themselves but is not rich toward God*" (Luke. 12:21).

Humanity's judgment of death, which accompanied sin, is reflected in the Apostle Paul's statement, "*Through one man sin entered the world, and death through sin*" (Rom.5:12). God allowed death to counteract sin because He did not create death nor is He the cause of transgression. Death emerged as a consequence of sin, as noted by the Apostle: "*When you were dead in your sins and in the un-circumcision of your flesh, God made you alive with Christ*" (Col.2:13). Now, death—through the cross and resurrection—serves as the force that destroys sin, as we consider ourselves "*dead to sin*" because we are crucified with Christ. We die to sin to live for righteousness. This represents our return to the "*original state,*" leaving behind the old, corrupted nature shaped by passions and desires. Death dismantles corrupt habits, but it is not merely "*death from sin*" but "*death with Jesus,*" a continual return to the cross, a life that rejects corrupt inclinations and wicked thoughts. We are no longer slaves to a nature but children who have received the grace of son-ship, a life united with Jesus Christ.
Death liberates the will. It is the cross's death that Jesus referred to when He said, "*Take up your cross*" (Luke 9:23). This on-going death, expressed as "*For*

Your sake we face death all day long" (Rom.8:36), requires us to bear the cross — our human life in all its forms — even those aspects that seem righteous, so they may be crucified. Through the cross, we gain a clear understanding of goodness and distinguish between good and evil. The cross represents the law of sacrifice, establishing fellowship. Fellowship reveals hidden corruption when we desire to take everything for ourselves and refuse to give.

Death also frees our emotions from selfishness. It exposes the corruption of greed, which the Apostle calls *"idolatry"* (Col.3:5). Through death, we recognize that our attachments, which nest in the heart, perish when tested against their true purpose and found to be non-eternal.

Furthermore, death liberates the mind from attachment to fleeting things. The memory of death is crucial as it strips away distractions, allowing the mind to be liberated. Even the memory of natural, biological death has its value, but the memory of our crucifixion with Jesus represents true freedom of thought.

The Cross as the Path to Spiritual Enlightenment

When seeking a truly beneficial *"medicine"* and a vital remedy that purifies the mind, we must reflect on the profound teachings of the crucified Jesus. This path of the cross is not merely a historical event but a spiritual journey for those who desire to crucify their own selves in union with Jesus. To pray through the cross, or to the crucified Jesus, involves more than mere words; it means allowing the profound messages of the Lord, as He hung on the cross, to become the foundation of our prayers. *Jesus, here I am, knocking at the door of life, yearning to walk with You along the path of the cross. I seek to be crucified*

But what role does the imagination play in this spiritual journey?

The imagination is an extraordinary power that acts as a mirror to the soul, capable of perceiving even the most profound heavenly matters. It allows us to grasp distant concepts with clarity and transforms nearby things into distant visions. When our heart is in harmony with Jesus, we perceive the Lord with the eyes of our hearts—through the imagination. This inner vision reveals Him standing with us, wiping away our pain and tears, and converting our suffering into a fervent, inner longing—a longing rooted in love. The eyes of the heart, guided by the imagination, are able to see the celestial realms and translate physical images into spiritual realities.

The imagination, through this process, gains a *"new vision"* derived from the symbols of new life revealed in the Bible. Jesus Christ, our Teacher of Truth, provided us with these sacred scriptures to open the eyes of our hearts to the new life He offers. He demonstrated this with the disciples on the road to Emmaus. Their hearts were set ablaze with the light of the Holy Spirit when He spoke to them and expounded on the scriptures. After teaching them, He sat with them, and as He broke the bread, their eyes were opened, and they recognized Him. This recognition was possible because their imagination had been purified by the word and by shared teaching. The rite of *"breaking bread"* moved them from the realm of the word to that of the *"sacrament,"* deepening their spiritual experience. The opening of their eyes represents a vision of the living Lord, a vision born from the word and the light of the Holy Spirit, enriched by the prelude of meeting the Lord on the road to Emmaus.

Prayers symbolically transport us, and through the word, to the sacramental encounter of the church with the Lord. It is crucial to understand that the Apostle Paul's references to the body and its members pertain to the sensory, visible world — our physical bodies. Yet, the deeper meanings are connected to the *"sacramental order"* because while the body is familiar, our collective fellowship in the Lord as members of one body reflects a heavenly revelation of unity between the Lord and His believers.

In prayer — symbolically — we open the eyes of the heart so that the heart, through the imagination, may perceive the profound mystery of the Lord's union with the body, that is, with us. The acceptance of this mystery is facilitated not just by the imagination, but by the illuminating light of the Holy Spirit. Revelation comes from God, much like fire; however, our responsibility is to place water in a vessel over the fire, symbolizing our partnership in God's work and revelation in Jesus Christ.

Thus, the imagination is liberated in two significant ways:
First, when it shifts from perceiving the tangible to the intangible, gaining an understanding of God's gift with spiritual insight. Second, when all the senses unite in the heavenly vision; for by tasting the heavenly bread and drinking the cup of His love, we transcend the tangible and visible through the gospel word, which we embrace in faith during prayers. This opens our eyes to witness the glory of the only Son

with the power and enlightenment granted by the Holy Spirit, according to our capacity.

Prayers, through their symbolism, transport us to the celestial realms. Facing the east during prayer stimulates spiritual attention. Raising hands symbolizes submission and acceptance of fellowship, and this gesture is described as the evening sacrifice, a voluntary offering in the service of Israel (Ps. 141:2). Bowing down represents a return to God's service and submission to His love through the Holy Spirit. Marking ourselves with the sign of the cross before beginning anything, simply by facing east, symbolizes our return to the seal of adoption and the anointing of baptism placed on our bodies with the life-giving cross. Lighting churches with candles and lamps, which signifies illuminating with the Holy Spirit's light, involves several aspects:

First, prayers help us move from laziness, slackness, and distraction by altering our bodily posture, such as raising hands or bowing, thereby unifying our inner and visible selves in heavenly service.

Second, symbols reveal the presence of the Lord Jesus and His divine nature and fellowship in our lives; for marking ourselves with the cross signifies our union with the Lord's cross in baptism, receiving the sacrament of His death and resurrection and becoming one with Him.

Thus, we begin prayers with the sign of fellowship, the honoured cross. Third, prayers guide us into the realm of the Holy Spirit's work; through the word and spiritual insight, we recognize that the power of our prayers comes from the Holy Spirit. Even through psalms and reading the holy gospel, our service aligns with the gospel and the call of the Holy Spirit. We worship in the Holy Spirit, guided by the revelations of the Holy Spirit and in truth, Jesus Christ our God. As we move, bow, or pray, the eyes of the heart perceive the reality of the revealed mystery from God the Father through His Son Jesus Christ by the Holy Spirit.

The Enduring Image of God and the Power of Spiritual Unity

Even in the midst of sin and moral failure, we retain our identity as the image and likeness of God. This truth is fundamental to our understanding of divine grace. God's grace, once given, does not diminish or dissipate, as He does not bestow it and then regret its application. The only regret God expresses, as described in the scriptures, pertains to the destruction of humanity rather than the loss of grace. The enduring presence of God's image within us is evidenced by the remarkable lives of holy figures from the Old Testament such as Abraham, Joseph, Elijah, and King Josiah. Their lives stand as profound examples of righteousness and divine reflection. Even amidst the pervasive idolatry and paganism seen throughout history, there have been individuals who, despite widespread cultural norms, resisted idolatry and guided people towards moral virtues — mirroring divine attributes like goodness, love, and justice.

The Apostle James reinforces this truth by stating that all humans are created in the image of God (James 3:9). This divine image was fully realized in the person of Jesus Christ, who is the Son of God and the image of the Father. Through His incarnation, Jesus manifested the true nature of this image, demonstrating how humanity can fully reflect divine attributes through a relationship with the Father. He showed that genuine fellowship and unity can only be restored by returning to God, the ultimate source of life and unity. Despite being equal to the Father in all respects and possessing the same divine attributes, Jesus lived His entire life oriented towards the Father. He accepted the Holy Spirit in His humanity for our sake and performed all His works, including miracles and exorcisms, through the power of the Holy Spirit. This perfect alignment and unity underscore the essence of divine fellowship.

Fellowship, in its truest form, reflects the ultimate truth that cannot exist in any form of separation or disunity. Separation is the first step toward spiritual fallenness, and death represents its ultimate consequence. Truth encompasses not only total surrender and complete participation but also embodies love that does not seek to benefit itself, as Paul writes: "*Love does not seek its own*" (1 Cor.13:5). True love is characterized by its ability to give and receive within an on-going cycle of life. Thus, our return to God is a return to fellowship — a restoration of all living members within the body of Christ, the Church, back to God. When we fail to maintain this fellowship, we revert to individualism, lacking the power and efficacy of collective unity, particularly in our ability to witness to those outside our faith.

Our prayers, fasting, praises, and all aspects of our spiritual life — including faith and confession — are manifestations of this fellowship. They represent human reflections of the divine image of complete, free, and authentic fellowship, as seen in the Holy Trinity. Failure to live in fellowship affects every facet of our lives, either overtly or subtly, impeding our witness and limiting the work of the Holy Spirit, who is the Spirit of fellowship. This does not imply that those who walk according to the Spirit are in any danger of losing grace. However, when the Church experiences weakness, the strength of any individual is a testament to God's grace, yet it highlights the weakness of the body as a whole. The absence of the Holy Spirit's gifts is not due to any fault of the Spirit, nor is it a matter of delayed grace, but rather a consequence of the disintegration of spiritual unity. When we do not live together as one body, each member may receive what is needed to sustain themselves in grace, but the whole body does not achieve the fullness of Christ's glory.

There is no precise law that dictates our obligations towards one another, other than the law embodied by Christ Jesus, who is Lord of all. He dwells in us and in others, so on the Day of Judgment, He will address everyone collectively rather than individually. Indeed, each person will find their place in the kingdom of our Lord Jesus Christ. However, failure to live out fellowship is a collective responsibility shared by those who have sown discord, remained silent when they should have testified, or engaged in actions that tear apart the unified body by rallying followers or opposing factions. Thus, the Lord's judgment encompasses everyone as a single body: "*Whatever you did to one of these least ones, you did to Me*" (Matt.25:40). We are judged together as one unified body. While individuals who fall will face the consequences of their actions, the general weakness affecting the whole body is apparent. Therefore, it is crucial for us to repent and return to God together, restoring our fellowship under one unified law: that the other is not only the inheritance of Christ but is Christ Himself.

We cannot fully detail how to treat others as we treat the Lord Jesus. The guiding principle is the absolute and perfect love that mirrors the love found in the Holy Trinity, which we strive to emulate through the grace of God working within us. We cannot embody the fellowship of the Trinity without the Trinity itself. Likewise, we cannot replicate the essence of the Trinity if the Trinity does not dwell within us. When Jesus promises that He, along with the Father and the Spirit, will come to dwell within us, it highlights that the Word who *was with the Father*" (John. 1:1) is the same Word who has brought us eternal life that is "*with the Father.*" This life was given to us not merely through words but through true fellowship granted by the Holy Spirit, enabling us to unite with the Lord Jesus through the narrow gate, which is the cross. When referring to the "*cross*," we mean not only the symbolic mark but also the King who embraced the cross as His personal attribute, being the Lamb of God sacrificed for the world's life so that we may live in and through Him. The cross thus becomes the seal of His love and His personal mark. As the cross serves as the *"joints"* that unify and mobilize all members of the body, it is clear that we are all crucified with Christ, and we all bear the cross in our hearts before marking it on our bodies. Even the sacred formula *"in the name of the Father, the Son, and the Holy Spirit"* reflects the essence of new birth. Through this formula, we are baptized, entering into a life of fellowship as members of one body. In baptism, the Lord plants the seed of His cross and nourishes it with the water of life, which is the Holy Spirit. This gift is given to all, making each of us Christ for the other, and the other Christ for us. This does not mean that the one Lord Jesus Christ is multiplied or fragmented; rather, the one life that connects us to the one Lord Jesus Christ is the life that was with the Father and has been given to us. It is through this divine life alone that we can live the new life by returning to God, the source of our existence.

Unity in the Church:
A Divine Gift and Collective Responsibility

We cannot achieve unity within the Church solely by our own efforts; true unity comes from above. It is a divine gift from the One who enables us to be one in Him. Christ, as the Head, provides the source from which all members grow together (Col.1:19). Our struggle, therefore, is not to create unity but to remain in it—remaining in grace. Our task is to transform our human nature from flesh and blood into spirit, a transformation made possible only through the power of the crucified Christ. While it is easy to convert spirit into flesh and become carnal, it is vital for our bodies to be spiritual to avoid repeating the fall of Adam. United with the Lord, we come to understand that everything in our earthly lives—food, drink, clothing, shelter, and money—should serve a higher purpose, which is to elevate us to the status of God's children. Carnal life begins when these necessities become ends in themselves, rather than means to a greater end. Jesus warned us of this when He said: *"Seek first the kingdom of God and His righteousness, and all these things will be added to you"* (Matt.6:33). Here, God's righteousness is not about the distribution of material goods but about subordinating all material needs to the single purpose of the kingdom of God.

The question then arises: How can we collectively repent or return to God? Returning to God is not merely about stopping sin, as some might believe, but about returning to the divine image within us, renewed through Christ Jesus. In Christ, we gain insight into the original Adam and understand his new, restored image, seeing how he was before the fall. This understanding alone does not purify us, nor is it helpful except to those who seek intellectual and philosophical insight. For those who yearn for the glory of Christ, the image of God in us is an image of freedom arising from love and sanctity, which is the result of our fellowship with God and with each other as Christians. This is manifested in Christ, who was free from the constraints of nature. By relinquishing His freedom, He demonstrated the freedom inherent in His Person. Through His sacrifice, He revealed divine love and sanctity, as seen in His role as High Priest *"called by God, not by men, according to the order of Melchizedek"* (Heb.6:5). His offering of Himself as a sacrifice to the Father not only provided life for us but also abolished death, making His sacrifice a gift for all who are united with Him *"in the likeness of His death"* (Rom.6:5). Thus, His resurrection, the first fruits of our new life, is the beginning of our own transformation. Without Him, we are nothing. As the Apostle Paul stated: *"For as many of you as were baptized into Christ have put on Christ"* (Gal.3:27). This shows us the path to return to God—returning to the divine image, which is the image of Christ within us.

Therefore, we must pray together, fast together, encourage one another, and avoid gossip and slander. We should always remember the Apostle's words: *"Love covers a multitude of sins"* (1 Peter.4:8). Our love for each other is the true sign of Christian living, leading us to seek what is good and beneficial for ourselves and for others.

The Cross as the Law of Love

When the Evangelist proclaimed that *"God is love,"* he decisively closed the door to any philosophical speculations regarding the nature and attributes of God. For any person capable of delving into the deepest mysteries of existence yet lacking love is, in truth, far removed from understanding or knowing God.

Jesus Christ's command to "*love your enemies*" firmly shut the door on all forms of religious practice and rituals, regardless of their complexity or reverence. This is because the love of one's enemies reflects God's love for all creation, irrespective of whether it acknowledges Him. It is a universal, encompassing love. Anyone who fails to exhibit this love does not comprehend the God who came to save us, even though we did not seek salvation, who redeemed us without any contribution from us, and who grants the kingdom freely. Thus, anyone lacking this kind of love has no inheritance with Christ, irrespective of their deeds.

Let us begin with love. If our love feels inadequate or weak, we should seek the Spirit of love (Rom.5:5) to receive the strength for a renewed life. Love has the power to dispel fear, and, by extension, it eliminates selfishness, which is a by-product of fear. Love, by its nature, willingly gives itself and thus achieves humility effortlessly; it does not boast or seek personal glory. Love forgives and cultivates peace with ease. It reconciles rather than creating enemies; even if there are many, love extends a hand of reconciliation, reducing their numbers gradually. Love guides faith, even though faith is its starting point, and it heals doubts with the soothing balm of hope. Love fosters a knowledge that aligns with faith, bringing tranquillity to understanding. Since love is inherently good, it transcends the law; the helm of love's ship is guided by the cross. Love, as the essence of fellowship, knows no boundaries; it births and strengthens fellowship continuously. Thus, love becomes the law for those who are complete.

Love transcends merely resisting sin; it is inherently about giving. Therefore, the repentance—or return—of those who love is marked by intense effort and sacrifice, not merely by tears and pleas. When they turn away from what they love, they experience the very terror of hell itself and swiftly return to God, the source of their love.

Love does not seek a codified set of rules for prayer but becomes prayer itself, for the essence of love is fellowship. If we ask how to involve the Lord Jesus in every action and thought, the answer is: *"Love the Lord with all your heart, mind, and will."* We understand this answer intuitively, don't we?

Love instils a special kind of understanding; it guides the heart to seek what is truly good and discerning in its requests for the benefit of fellowship. It shuns doubt, as doubt depletes its true power and hinders its effectiveness. Love casts aside doubt with the strength of hope, for the primary proof of love is God's gift, and the ultimate proof is the inheritance of the kingdom.

Since God is love, and love is the divine law, and everything revealed in the Scriptures should be understood through the lens of love's revelation, namely Jesus Christ, love does not engage in debates over the precise meanings of words but comprehends their ultimate purpose. Love does not argue over individual terms but seeks wisdom. It avoids setting boundaries that create discord. It preserves the divine mystery in Christ effortlessly, bound by one law —the cross. It answers even the devil's provocations without difficulty, not to convert or redirect him but to present him with the shield of humility, causing him to flee. When the devil appears as an angel of light, love discerns the pride and arrogance behind the facade and mocks it. If an unbeliever seeks answers about the incarnation, the Trinity, or the cross, love responds with faith-filled words and can distinguish between those seeking genuine knowledge and those looking for a contentious debate.

Why do we assert that the cross is the law of love? Because the cross exemplified the true essence of sacrifice for those who did not deserve it and for those who did not ask or seek it. It provided forgiveness to those who did not plead for it. It opened the gates of paradise to those who had no hope but received far more than they could have imagined. It transformed death, the fruit of sin, to destroy sin itself and removed the curse of death. The crucified's command, *"Bless and do not curse"* (Rom.12:14), became the path to righteousness. The cross demolished the power of hell and eradicated it, overturning judgment and allowing mercy to triumph over condemnation (James. 2:13). From the cross, blood and water flowed from the Lord's side, symbolizing purification and salvation through baptism for all who seek it. The cross tore up the debt of condemnation and nailed all the judgments of the law, making every commandment regarding human behaviour a manifestation of love. Thus, the law of Moses was surpassed as it was written on the human heart with the blood of Jesus Christ, establishing a new and eternal law of love.

The Role of Discernment in Love

Love fundamentally requires discernment, which forms the foundation of all virtues. However, it is crucial to ensure that discernment does not overshadow or detract from love. Discernment should not hinder those who seek Jesus with a sincere heart. While discernment is essential for understanding goodness, it is inherently linked to love, and love cannot flourish without it.

Discernment aids faith in distinguishing between true and false teachings by reflecting God's love for humanity. Any doctrine that denies or diminishes this love is of demonic origin. The Apostle John warned us against false prophets who deny that Jesus Christ came in the flesh. The incarnation of the Son of God should be the guiding principle of discernment, enabling us to reject false teachings that undermine God's profound love for humanity.

Furthermore, love discerns the doctrine of bodily resurrection, not solely because of Jesus Christ's resurrection but also because the resurrection serves as God's affirmation of His love for both body and soul. This divine love confirms the totality of human existence.

Love also discerns the correct interpretation of the Scriptures, based on the faith we have received and profess in our prayers. An interpretation that aligns with the creed is considered accurate, even if the specific wording differs. The diversity in expression reflects the freedom of God's children and underscores the ultimate goal of all interpretation: salvation.

Different interpretations of a single text do not undermine salvation. However, interpretations that deny the dignity of son-ship or bind humanity with doubts about God's goodness are unacceptable, as they contradict our love for God and His love for us, which is unified and unwavering.

Prayers and services are means to an end, not ends themselves. They are structures designed to maintain order and support faith and love, without restricting God's grace but seeking its revelation. As the Lord stated, the Sabbath was made for man, thus placing man above the commandment. Those who experience God's love understand this, whereas those bound by rigid laws and rituals may elevate the commandment above humanity, failing to recognize that *"the Lord of the Sabbath,"* Jesus Christ, made man superior to the commandment by becoming incarnate for us. As one *"full of grace and truth,"* He is acknowledged as the Son of God and the Lord of the Sabbath.

The Apostle Paul affirms, *"There is one mediator between God and man, Jesus Christ, who gave Himself as a ransom for us"* (1 Tim.2:5). He is not merely another prophet who came to reveal the Father's will; He is the only Son of the Father and the sole mediator between God and humanity. Faith identifies and rejects all other mediators. Love also discerns and rejects any foreign redemption or denial of the cross, as it cannot recognize true knowledge. Humanity cannot redeem itself, sanctify its being, or love its enemies through its own power. Those who deny that the message of the cross is *"the power of God for salvation"* are lacking in discernment, faith, and love, as they do not grasp the essence of goodness or possess hope in eternal life.

Oppression, domination, and fear are traits associated with the devil. Domination denies the incarnation, oppression rejects the crucified, and fear rejects love. Thus, those who discern these three elements, which often appear united, possess faith and discernment. Those who teach to gather followers seek power like their father, the devil; those who use fear seek power like their master, the devil, and burden people with heavy loads, similar to the Jewish rulers, while being too proud to share in these burdens.

There is only one sacred fear known to all: the fear in faith. The hallmark of this fear is adherence to the commandments. Other fears have no place in our lives. We discern fear in faith by seeking its purpose, as it is written, *"The fear of the Lord is the beginning of wisdom"* (Prov.9:10).

Three types of doubts exist: doubts arising from a lack of knowledge, doubts stemming from a weakness in love, and doubts due to a lack of upright faith. The first type can be addressed through studying the Scriptures and seeking guidance. The second can be remedied by seeking the help of the Holy Spirit. The third requires a more radical approach, as a lack of faith is treated by rejecting temporal and earthly concerns, which may lead to doubts about the commandments and God's mercy and love.

Before addressing doubts, we must understand their purpose. Doubts about God's love differ from doubts about the wisdom and efficacy of the Gospel's commandments. Those who discern the purpose of their doubts will navigate life more calmly and with less struggle than those who debate their doubts.

Doubt that undermines the necessity of returning to God, or repentance, signifies the beginning of a hardened heart and the death of love. This condition is critical and requires the remedy of knowledge and communal prayers, as failing to repent signifies spiritual death.

Those who seek love from the Trinity live in communion with the Trinity and through the Trinity. Those who seek discernment from the Trinity master the art of fellowship and understand their place with the heavenly Father. Through love, we enter the depths of the Trinity, which is the fellowship of love. Through discernment, we realize that our fellowship is by grace, with our assurance being our High Priest, the Lord Jesus Christ.

The Essential Role of Service in Spiritual Growth

Service represents a fundamental pillar for anyone aspiring to enter the Kingdom of Heaven, as it is powered by the strength and grace of the Trinity. To serve those in need is to mirror the divine nature of the Lord Himself. Serving at tables, for example, symbolizes our shared responsibility in God's on-going care for creation. After all, it is God who plants the seeds, waters the earth, and provides both the crops and the harvest (Ps.147).

In the same way that fasting, prayer, and church fellowship help cleanse the heart from excessive self-centeredness, service plays a crucial role. Visiting the sick and caring for the elderly allows us to confront our own mortality and shift our reliance away from mere physical strength.

Each person should choose a form of service that aligns with their personal inclinations and skills. However, there are times when we must engage in forms of service that do not necessarily appeal to us in order to truly discover the depth of our love and inner peace. Avoiding service might sometimes be motivated by personal concerns or interests that conflict with the commandments of the Lord.

Rather than pursuing a specific type of service based merely on personal preference, it is important to seek the Lord's guidance through prayer. Jesus, who serves us continuously, is our model. By entering into service through prayer and unity with Him, we learn much about ourselves and enhance our spiritual purity.

Engagement with Scripture through reading and study is essential for everyone. Those who have been gifted with the ability to teach should not shy away from serving others, especially the sick and needy. Jesus, who both taught and acted, set the standard; those who teach but do not practice should critically examine their own hearts to ensure that pride does not silently undermine their intentions.

The true, living icon of Christ is found in those whom we serve, and this is far more profound than any painted image. The glory of the Lord is not confined to illustrations, wood, or colours; it is manifested in humanity, which is made in the image and likeness of God.

A genuine longing to serve the church reflects a deeper yearning for heavenly things. However, the true church of the Lord Jesus is found in the individuals who are in need of service and mercy. Acts of love and kindness carry a glory that transcends the temporary value of earthly service garments, which will eventually decay.

In our prayers, we invoke the Holy Spirit with expressions of sincere devotion. Acts of mercy are manifestations of the Holy Spirit working through us, allowing Him to dwell within us and in others.

If we wish to contribute a living chapter to the Scriptures, we can do so through our service to others. This act of service can reveal something akin to the experiences recorded in the Acts of the Apostles, or it can bring to light the Lord's glory as He performs miracles of faith through us.

Jesus said, "*I was sick, naked, imprisoned, and in need, and you came and served my needs.*" If we genuinely desire to be deified by the Holy Spirit, we have the opportunity to enter into communion with the divine nature at any time. Jesus identified with the sick, the naked, and the imprisoned because He became one with us, gathering us into His holy person. As the Apostle states, "*He is not ashamed to call them brothers*" (Heb.2:11). If we profess to believe this yet fail to serve those in need, our faith becomes insubstantial and disconnected from its true purpose.

Our return to God through prayer, fasting, church fellowship, and service are the cornerstones of eternal life. Eternal life itself is a divine gift from God the Father, revealed to us through Jesus Christ and supported by the guidance of the Holy Spirit. Our words and actions are not the sources of grace; rather, grace is embodied in Jesus Christ, who came in the last days to offer us a life we do not deserve, thereby uprooting the prideful roots that might otherwise hinder our spiritual growth.

True Repentance:
The Necessity of Genuine Love

Repentance, in its truest form, cannot exist without genuine love. A repentance that is merely motivated by fear lacks the deep, self-sacrificial essence of true love. When repentance is driven solely by the fear of punishment, it results in a superficial change that is not truly transformative. This kind of repentance may lead to temporary remorse but fails to bring about a profound and lasting transformation in the heart.

Every moment offers an opportunity for repentance, and those who practice repentance regularly will find their love continually growing. Persistent sin often signals that love has not yet fully matured, as repeated failures reveal a weakness of will and an overpowering of personal desires. Such desires indicate a self-centred love that has not been fully penetrated by the profound love of the crucified Jesus, nor has the cross truly impacted its depths.

A person who, after falling, rises up with a heart full of genuine love will be able to maintain their spiritual standing. On the other hand, if one is driven merely by remorse, there is a risk of falling repeatedly, as true repentance involves more than a fear of punishment; it involves recognizing the loss of communion with the Trinity. This deeper understanding of repentance emphasizes the need for a transformation that goes beyond mere regret.

Repentance motivated by fear is not a genuine repentance but a form of regret. Regret alone does not cultivate or sustain love. The true nourishment for a repentant heart comes from the living water provided by the Holy Spirit, who brings comfort and renewal. The Holy Spirit alone can invigorate and sustain the love that true repentance requires.

Instead of seeking excuses for any fall, which reflects a lack of true repentance, we should be ready to accept excuses from others, regardless of their nature, as this demonstrates humility. The readiness to forgive others reflects a deeper understanding of true repentance and the humility it requires.

Address the Lord Jesus with your confessions: *"I have sinned against Your incarnation by failing to honour Your body. I have sinned against Your cross by clinging to what I love. I have sinned against Your resurrection by prioritizing earthly pleasures over heavenly glory."* In response, you will receive comfort from Him, as He affirms that He became incarnate for you and was sacrificed for your sake. His unwavering love led Him to rise from the dead to redeem your body from decay and death.

For those seeking an apostolic path to repentance, the route is through prayer to Jesus. Make Jesus your prayer, allowing this prayer to guide you into a life of true communion. Pray for His incarnation, His baptism, His temptations in the wilderness, His teachings, His redemptive death, and His resurrection. By embracing these aspects, you will walk the true path of repentance and experience a deeper spiritual transformation.

Your faith should either crucify all your sins, allowing you to live entirely for Jesus, or your sins should crucify your faith, leading to spiritual death.

True repentance involves a transformation that aligns your actions with your faith.

Let love triumph over all fears so that your faith can thrive. If fear—particularly the hidden fear of death—continues to conflict with love, it will weaken your faith. Engage your fears with faith, and you will find them powerless. When love inspires your faith and your faith nurtures your love, you will find yourself on the path of life, with your fears rendered ineffective.

Sorrow naturally accompanies genuine repentance, but forgiveness brings about joy. Seek forgiveness not merely to escape the punishment of sin but to restore your communion with the Trinity: the Father, the Son, and the Holy Spirit. This restoration to divine fellowship is the true goal of repentance.

The real punishment for sin is not from God but is manifested in fear, doubt, loss of hope, and estrangement from those we have wronged. These are the true consequences of sin.

To avoid the true punishment of sin, cling to faith and the living promises of the Heavenly Father, sealed by His Son Jesus Christ and the Holy Spirit. This is where true hope and redemption lie.

Sin does not merely affect specific parts of the body or mind but originates from the heart and impacts all aspects of our being. Those who blame the body as the source of sin have not genuinely repented, as they fail to recognize that sin stems from a separation from communion, a lack of faith, and the dominance of desires over the heart and mind.

Sins such as lying, gossiping, and cursing reflect a heart devoid of the peace and joy of the Holy Spirit. Therefore, before you train yourself to speak kindly and avoid lying, align yourself with the Spirit of Truth to resonate with the truth spoken by the Holy Spirit. This alignment is crucial for true repentance.

Regarding the cessation of lying: first, repent of fear and crucify its root—pride. Both fear and pride indicate a lack of union with the crucified Jesus, who is the true Lord of repentance and the healer of hearts through love. This process of repentance and healing is essential for true spiritual growth and transformation.

The Path to True Repentance: Moving Beyond Self-Love

Understand deeply that true repentance is impossible if you continue to excessively love yourself. If your self-love surpasses your love for God, genuine repentance remains elusive. The reason is that the Son of God came to earth and poured out His life as a living sacrifice to God the Father, creating a path to life for those who, through repentance, choose to partake in the sacrificial journey of the cross alongside Him.

Nothing can remove pride from the heart except the one who emptied Himself and died on the cross. By assuming the *"form of a servant,"* He laid the first cornerstone of repentance by completely discarding pride. When those who do not believe belittle the significance of the cross of our Lord, they undermine the very foundation of repentance. This results in a superficial form of repentance, similar to a blind person spinning in circles, mistakenly believing they are journeying towards a peaceful realm.

Do not leave your heart like a barren land or an unprotected field. Man, created in the image of God, is meant to be a reflection of the Word, the Son of God. We are called to follow Him with the strength of the original grace—the gift of being created in God's image. If one follows Him out of ignorance or disbelief, they will not reach the promised land of peace and the harbour of salvation, which is true faith in the Lord Jesus Christ.

True humility does not instil a fear of death or the fires of hell. Fear, which is born from its hidden mother — pride — produces impurity, self-exaltation, and domination. How can fear produce humility when its mother, pride, wields such power and continuously aligns itself with forces that generate the offspring of the devil?

The Son of God cultivates humility through His own example. He abandoned His glory and embraced humiliation, accepted weakness despite His inherent strength, and triumphed over death by openly disarming it on the cross. He approaches the soul, planting the seed of faith in the heart, which eventually yields genuine humility.

You might wonder about the difference between true humility and false humility. True humility originates from Jesus, the Lord of life, while false humility is a creation of the devil. When you remove the façade of false humility, you will discover underneath a desire for power, control, and the subjugation of others, along with a pretence of virtues such as gentle speech, cheerfulness, and hospitality — all designed to attract positive attention. Conversely, when dealing with someone who is falsely humble, you may find them reacting with harshness and cruelty, leaving no room for apologies. Even if you offer an apology, they may not accept it and may publicly shame you, as their love for power reflects the same vice found in the devil.

If you miss an opportunity to sin and experience regret and sorrow, you have not yet achieved pure repentance. This regret indicates that you still harbour a love for sin and that your repentance remains at a nascent stage.

The Apostle teaches us that "*love does not rejoice in wrongdoing,*" a principle that opposes taking pleasure in or delighting in the failures of others. Those who publicly shame the fallen are allies of the devil, finding comfort in recalling others' sins to deflect attention from their own.

When the Apostle says that "*love never fails,*" he refers to God's unwavering love for us. As stated in Romans 5:8, "*While we were still sinners, Christ died for us,*" affirming that "*God demonstrated His love for us.*" This declaration should not be read hastily but should be pondered deeply to understand the divine love that remains constant when we repent and does not weaken when we falter, remaining always as a living flame of divine presence.

When the Apostle states, "*There is no fear in love*" (1 John. 4:18), he implies that repentance should not be driven solely by fear. While fear can be a motivating factor to turn towards God, if fear remains the primary force guiding us, we have not fully embraced true faith.

Do not imitate the behaviour of immature individuals who repent only to avoid causing sadness to God's heart. Instead, adopt the behaviour of mature individuals who repent out of genuine love for God.

It is essential to understand that God does not need our repentance; rather, we need repentance as it is the path to eternal life. Thus, repentance should be pursued for the sake of attaining everlasting life.

At the outset of the Gospel, the Lord proclaimed, "*Repent and believe in the Gospel*" (Mark. 1:15). He brought the good news and the promise of life, which includes the acceptance of those who repent. Therefore, every time we read the Gospel in church, we should remember this vital beginning to keep our hope strong and unshakable.

Repentance:
The Gateway to New Life in Christ

You might wonder why we didn't begin by defining repentance. The reason is that repentance is the gateway to a new and transformative life in Jesus Christ. Defining repentance alone does not enable one to repent, much like buying a fishing rod does not guarantee catching fish without the necessary practice of sitting by the river, casting bait, and patiently waiting. Repentance is not merely a concept but a journey and a practice that requires commitment and understanding.

Knowledge is indeed essential for everyone, but it must be subordinated to faith. Just as a servant submits to his master, our understanding must yield to faith. Faith acts as the master that directs and commands our thoughts and actions. The Apostle Paul highlights this by referring to "*the obedience of faith*" (Rom.1:5), indicating that our thoughts and minds must align with and be governed by faith. This submission ensures that our understanding serves a higher purpose and guides us on the path to genuine repentance.

Repentance without the cross is akin to filling one's stomach with water and mistakenly believing that it is the only necessary sustenance for life. Such repentance is hollow and incomplete because the cross represents the true remedy that offers us abundant, eternal life. The cross is the source from which we receive the fruit of the Tree of Life, symbolized by the body and blood of Christ. This life-giving sustenance is integral to true repentance, as it provides the nourishment necessary for spiritual growth and renewal.

Should we attend church and engage in prayers if we have doubts about the sincerity of our repentance? The answer is a resounding yes. As the Lord Himself said, "*It is not the healthy who need a doctor, but the sick*" (Matt.9:12). We should approach church with faith and hope, regardless of our personal feelings or doubts. The Lord's compassion and love extend to all, including sinners. By choosing to dine with tax collectors and sinners, Jesus established the Church's role in offering healing and redemption. His presence among us signifies that we should approach with faith, irrespective of our emotional state, because drawing near to the Lord grants us His life and helps us truly live. Believing we can achieve this without Him shows a lack of understanding of the fact that He is the ultimate source of life.

It is crucial to confess your sins directly to the Lord before seeking advice from a spiritual guide. When you confess to the Lord, you are revealing your innermost self to the Saviour, who alone has the power to restore and renew your life. This direct confession is a step toward healing and receiving the grace necessary for genuine repentance.

Regret arising from love is fundamentally different from regret born out of fear. Regret that comes from love carries promises of true life and transformation, whereas regret that stems from fear is often tied to apprehensions of judgment. Love motivates the heart to draw closer to God with hope in His divine goodness, as revealed through Jesus Christ and the gift of the Holy Spirit. On the other hand, fear drives the heart away, with dread of judgment obscuring the understanding of God's goodness and making the purpose of His commandments unclear. Regret rooted in love leads to true, life-giving repentance, while regret born of fear is more connected to the law and judgment.

Genuine regret produces tears—tears of someone who recognizes their loss of place as a child of God and a sibling among many brethren (Rom.8:29). Many have experienced profound cleansing and renewal through such tears. However, the gift of tears alone does not instil God's love within us; rather, God's love is a gift of the Holy Spirit and comes with urgency and the transformative power of the cross applied in our hearts.

Seeking tears for their own sake is not fruitful; they naturally flow as a result of contemplating God's goodness and His deep compassion. Abundant weeping can cleanse the heart, but true sanctification requires the aid of the Comforter. Sanctity is not achieved through our own efforts or good deeds but is a divine gift from the Holy Spirit. While prayers and good works are important, they are like preparing the soil; it is the seed and water that bring life and yield the harvest. The seed represents the living word of God found in the Scriptures, and life itself is given by the Spirit of Jesus, who longs to sanctify and renew us.

Remembering past sins is not beneficial for those who have not yet tasted the profound love of God. In fact, it can be harmful and counterproductive. A wise teacher focuses on the positive aspects of learning rather than dwelling on past mistakes. This approach encourages growth and understanding rather than fostering guilt and regret.

Rebuking others, even if they have committed significant sins in your presence, should be done with caution and only if you have an established relationship with them. Rebuke can be like a spark that ignites widespread destruction if not handled with care. If you lose a brother due to harsh rebuke, it becomes challenging to guide him back to Christ, the true healer.

What about pride? Can we truly repent of pride? Pride is like a venomous snake that hides within the heart. Destroying its den may make us think we have eradicated it, but only the genuine spirit of humility—emulating Christ, who humbled Himself and took on the form of a servant—can truly conquer pride. Humility is the antidote to pride and the foundation for authentic repentance.

Avoid engaging in arguments with those who thrive on contention, as pride often lurks in their hearts. The Apostle James advises, "*Do not be eager to become teachers*" (James. 3:1) because we all stumble in many ways. Engaging in fruitless debates can exacerbate pride and hinder spiritual growth.

Regular reading of the Scriptures is essential, as they serve as the waters that cleanse the heart of impurity and expose the hidden pride within. The Scriptures illuminate the path to true repentance and help reveal areas where pride may still reside.

Pride drives us to pursue fleeting and superficial goals, believing they hold the essence of life. With pride comes the fear of death and the uncertainty it brings. The timid and indecisive struggle with true repentance; the timid fear the sacrifice of the cross, while the indecisive fear the discomfort of love.

Therefore, we must embody the courage of a lion, who knows how to pursue and strike its prey with precision. True repentance requires bravery and determination. When we cast wood into the fire, it burns more intensely with each additional piece. Similarly, recognizing our true worth before God increases the fervour and intensity of our repentance. If we allow "*smallness of heart*" to prevail, it cools the flames of repentance and hinders our spiritual growth.

True dignity and worth come not from external praise but from understanding that the Son of God, beloved of the Father, sacrificed Himself for us. This profound realization is what imbues us with genuine dignity and worth.

Contrition arises not from merely cataloguing sins or from reprimands but from recognizing the futility of evil and the sweetness of God's love — the love of a Father who gave His only Son for our sake and bestowed upon us His Holy Spirit.

Contrition sustains repentance because it fosters a continuous yearning and cry for the Lord's mercy. It instils in us a hopeful plea to the Saviour, who alone possesses the remedy for eternal life and the power to heal our ailing human nature.

Those who seek human praise often find the path to repentance very narrow; they are unwilling to turn away from public sins and continue to indulge in them to preserve their false, superficial status before God. True repentance requires a willingness to abandon such false facades and embrace genuine spiritual renewal.

The Role of the Holy Spirit in True Repentance

True spiritual joy in the Lord and the inheritance of the kingdom of God is reflected in a joyful countenance rather than a sombre one. Genuine repentance does not lead to a gloomy expression but rather to an inner peace and happiness. Even when we stumble, the sorrow we experience comes from a sense of lost fellowship with God. This sorrow is not due to mere reprimand but is addressed through the comforting presence of the Holy Spirit, who instils hope and reassurance in God's goodness and love.

Unlike judges or masters who impose their authority with a sense of finality and control, the Holy Spirit interacts with sinners in a manner akin to a compassionate healer. Rather than delivering judgment, the Holy Spirit provides a diagnosis of spiritual ailments with kindness and empathy, offering a remedy and promising eventual healing. This is in contrast to our own tendencies to judge harshly without offering solutions or proclaiming God's promises. Sometimes, the desire for control can overshadow our faith in God's promises, leading us to focus on authority rather than on healing and restoration.

The intercession and work of the Holy Spirit are tailored to fit the spiritual needs and growth of each individual believer. There are no rigid protocols or specific rules governing the Holy Spirit's work; rather, His influence is profound yet gentle, cultivating perseverance and faith in Christ without exerting dominance. The Holy Spirit's role is not to impose but to nurture, guiding the believer with a spirit of gentleness and understanding.

For example, the Holy Spirit's intercession involves speaking to the believer's heart with divine wisdom and revelation. He offers gentle correction while filling the soul with peace and joy, avoiding any sense of oppression or tyranny. His comfort comes through God's living promises, and He remains with the soul, providing encouragement and solace. The Holy Spirit's influence is so seamless that the believer may feel as though they are having an internal dialogue with themselves. When believers maintain their fellowship with God, the Holy Spirit strengthens them to endure the trials of life. Conversely, when a believer falls into sin, they may experience a period of spiritual darkness, reflective of the intensity of their desires and transgressions. As the fleeting pleasure of sin dissipates and the individual awakens from this spiritual stupor, the Holy Spirit approaches quietly and gently. He addresses the soul with insights into the futility of sin and how it has corrupted their inner life. In these moments, the Holy Spirit acts as a skilled physician, revealing the nature of the spiritual illness and offering the cure. He tenderly reminds the soul of its first love, the prayers, and the worship that once brought strength and comfort. The Holy Spirit helps revive the seed of hope through reminders of past celebrations and promises, reopening the path to renewed spiritual vitality.

Jesus referred to the Holy Spirit as the *"Paraclete,"* a term meaning the advocate or helper. Unlike a legal defence attorney, the Holy Spirit offers guidance and mentorship, embodying the unity of the Trinity's goodness and comfort. The Holy Spirit, understanding the depths of the human soul, operates like a nurturing teacher. He explains God's promises, reveals the mysteries of heavenly life, and offers a foretaste of this life so that the soul may live in hope and freely let go of the pleasures, desires, and vanities associated with sin.

Ultimately, the Holy Spirit's role is to preserve and fortify the soul within Christ, ensuring that it remains steadfast in the Lord's commandments and does not underestimate the seriousness of sin. The Holy Spirit's work is not merely about correction but about nurturing a genuine transformation and renewal that aligns the believer with the divine will and purpose.

The Death of Sin:
Rejection of Grace and Denial of Christ

The death of sin represents a profound and critical departure from God's grace, a rejection of our faith, and a denial of our Lord Jesus Christ. This concept underscores the severe consequences of losing touch with divine grace and how it impacts our spiritual journey.

The onset of sin's death can be compared to the gradual cooling of water. Just as water slowly loses its warmth until it becomes cold, so too does the heart's love gradually grow cold. Jesus, the Teacher of Life, warned us about this phenomenon, stating, *"Because of the increase of wickedness, the love of most will grow cold"* (Matt.24:12). This cooling of love signals the beginning of a profound spiritual decline.

Despite this dire warning, there is no need for fear. We have a compassionate Saviour, the Son of the Father, to whom we turn with the assurance that *"Your holy name is our confession."* By acknowledging and holding onto Him as the *"Author of Life,"* we align ourselves with the very source of spiritual vitality and renewal. Through the power of the Holy Spirit, our souls are revived, and we can confidently assert that *"the death of sin cannot prevail against us."* This vitality comes from our continued connection with the source of life, which counters the coldness of sin.

The process of sin's death begins with the gradual cooling of love and can be accelerated by various factors. When divine commandments are mixed with worldly standards, when heavenly comfort is overshadowed by temporary hopes, and when the temptations of sin become alluring, there is a risk of an initial denial of the Lord within the heart before this denial becomes evident in our outward actions.

The signs that sin has begun to take hold are unmistakable. They include a growing indifference towards and resistance to God's commandments, a disregard for the teachings found in the scriptures, and the acceptance of worldly standards as the new measure of truth. Additionally, hatred and contempt for Jesus and a disregard for His cross become evident. All these signs point to a deeper issue encapsulated in the phrase: *"coldness of love."*

The path of heresy, as orchestrated by the devil, begins with teachings that deny the incarnation of the Son of God, who is equal to the Father. It rejects the union of the Son with complete human nature — both soul and body. Such teachings obscure and ultimately destroy our need for divine life, which is essential for eternal existence. The incarnate Son, who mediates between us and the Father, offers a new path to renewed life. Heresy undermines the humility of God and His acceptance of the incarnation, distorting His love by denying His union with us and the gift of eternal life. It confines this union to merely the divinity and humanity of our Lord Jesus Christ while isolating Him as the sole source of eternal life.

Consequently, prayers lose their effectiveness, repentance becomes constrained by human effort alone, and the gift of eternal life is relegated to those who, through their own efforts, seek the divine source of unending life. This is the essence of the evil inherent in unbelief: a denial of the fundamental truths of our faith and a rejection of the transformative power of divine grace. The result is a diminished spiritual vitality and a disconnection from the life-giving presence of Christ, which ultimately leads to a more profound and perilous spiritual death.

The Divine Gift Preserved by the Holy Trinity

The divine gift from God is safeguarded through the practices of fasting, prayer, reading the holy scriptures, and active participation in the Church. However, this divine gift does not originate from these practices alone. Instead, it comes directly from the Holy Trinity: from the Father through the Son and by the grace of the Holy Spirit. Therefore, true repentance is impossible without the involvement of the Trinity. We must be vigilant against any teachings that attempt to place repentance outside the framework of the Trinity, for without the Trinity, we cannot be regarded as children of God but only as children of the flesh. Without the Trinity, we have no part in divine life, because if we do not receive the Holy Spirit, we face eternal death, which causes the life within us to wither and perish. By our nature, created from nothing, we are incapable of living forever without divine intervention.

While the explanation provided thus far is substantial, it is essential to delve deeper into God's plan that has provided us the path to life through Jesus Christ and established this path within us through the Son and the Holy Spirit. The incarnation of the Son of God marked the beginning of the proclamation of life. The Holy Spirit prepared the human vessel that the incarnate Son, our Lord Jesus Christ, would inhabit. This was not merely a matter of the Son dwelling in a human form; it was a profound union, as affirmed by the sacred words: *"His divinity did not separate from His humanity for a single moment, nor the twinkling of an eye."* Jesus was not God at certain times and human at others; rather, He is the incarnate Son of God, permanently united with human nature. In Him, human nature is glorified with the richness and majesty of divinity.

Thus, true repentance begins with the incarnation of the Son of God, which established humility as the foundation of our communion with God. This humility is characterized not by a display of power but by a humble love that triumphs over death through weakness, destroys pride through meekness, and restores life through love. This essence of unity with the Lord Jesus indicates that genuine repentance starts with the humility of the incarnate Christ, who did not use power to achieve victory but *"emptied Himself."* This self-emptying is a fundamental aspect of the incarnation, followed by the stumbling block of the cross — an offering of life to those who did not seek it and to those who did not deserve it, namely, humanity that crucified the Lord of Glory. The self-emptying came before the offering, and self-emptying was completed through death. Thus, by weakness, Christ overcame death and demolished its stronghold through His crucifixion. Therefore, repentance begins with humility, self-emptying, sacrifice, and the rejection of power.

The persistent urging of the Holy Spirit in our hearts is noteworthy; He leads us gently toward the cross. He opens our hearts to release our attachment to the present life in all its forms, allowing us to place this life entirely at the feet of Christ. He comforts us by revealing the beauty of heavenly promises, assuring us that heaven is better, that the spirit is more significant than the body, and that fellowship with God surpasses all earthly treasures. This persistent urging, which we experience daily, draws us back to repentance. Because of our fellowship in Christ, the Holy Spirit approaches us with tenderness and goodness, working within us to convey from the Lord all that pertains to His goodness and love shown toward sinners and the fallen, instilling in us a hope that does not perish.

The signs of the Holy Spirit's presence within us include hope and trust in God's goodness and His acceptance of sinners. Sin, due to the pride within us, leads us toward despair—reminiscent of the sin of Judas Iscariot. The Holy Spirit gently guides us toward the crucified Jesus, embedding the cross in our thoughts, hearts, and wills. In the mind, as a vision; in the heart, as a deep love that motivates the will toward forgiveness and sacrifice; and in the will, to reject not only the temptations of sin but even the good things that hinder self-sacrifice.

The Holy Spirit leads us to Jesus crucified to grant us Christian repentance—that is, the repentance of those who, in Christ, have been anointed with the Holy Spirit. According to this anointing, which is of the crucified and living One who transformed death into life and the tomb into rest, we receive the death of the old life in Christ and, in Him, the indwelling Spirit of life who raised Jesus from the dead. Repentance represents a resurrection from death, not by our own power but through the power of Jesus Christ. True repentance, empowered by the anointing, is driven forcefully toward the cross as the law of life. Repentance driven solely by willpower, on the other hand, seeks out every excuse and cause of sin, pursuing and trampling them without hesitation. The former is the fire of love; the latter is the rain that waters the parched earth.

When the will, along with the mind and heart, searches the desert of repentance for the power of new life and finds none within, it becomes like a thirsty soul gasping for a single drop of water. This marks the beginning of new life and the womb from which we are all born. The Lord leads us in the wilderness toward the unending fountain of water, which always overflows—the Holy Spirit, the Lord and Life-giver, who brings us the life of the Lord

Jesus sealed with the cross, crowned with resurrection, and glorified with ascension.

Repentance without suffering is not genuine. This does not merely refer to the loss of pleasures of the old life but to the suffering described by the Apostle: "*The world has been crucified to me, and I to the world*" (Gal.2:20). It is the Holy Spirit who crucifies us with the Lord, anointed after baptism with the chrism to partake in the sufferings of the Lord: the nails, the thorns, and the beatings — symbolizing the world's afflictions to achieve the death of the old life. The futility of the world has been revealed through its powerlessness, and the corruption of authority that does not know love has been exposed. The Lord established love through the humility of His incarnation and the outpouring of His sacrificial love on the cross, which, through resurrection, became the eternal victory of life over death and love over enmity.

Thus, "*the Spirit of Jesus*" dwells within us, instilling in us the incarnation of the Son of God with the humility of the incarnate One, the death of the life-giving Lord — that is, the cross — and the life that overcomes death and corruption, namely, the resurrection. We experience genuine repentance not by denying ourselves in the emptiness of sin but by seeing ourselves as if in a mirror, recognizing our flaws while seeing the image of Christ. The mirror here is Christ Jesus, our Lord, and when we see Him as He is, we leave our old life. When we see our divided love, we leave it. When we recognize the filth of the life within us, we seek His purity. Thus, the Holy Spirit works, moving us toward the crucified and living One for eternity.

Our Lord said: "*If anyone wants to be my disciple, he must deny himself and take up his cross and follow me*" (Luke. 9:23). He is the leader and true shepherd of the Church, calling us to carry our cross, our life given in sacrifice, and follow Him. Only by walking with the Lord and sharing in His sufferings do we reach Golgotha, where the Lord crucified humanity so that we might die with Him to the old life. Did the Lord have an old life? Certainly not, but it was and remains our life in Him—the life He recreated in Himself, which was deified by union and glorified with the fullness of divinity. This life has been transformed into humility and complete surrender to the Father and anointed with the Holy Spirit to preserve this anointing for us. Therefore, all the work of the Holy Spirit in us during our time of exile is to transform us into the image of Christ. The Holy Spirit moves us toward the Lord in prayer, in reading the scriptures, in serving love among our brethren, and in leaving behind all that contradicts His commandments.

Understanding True Humility and the Role of Confession in Spiritual Renewal

When considering humility, it is essential to grasp that true humility is not merely about uttering the phrase "*I am a sinner*" or attempting to feel remorse for one's sins, especially when we might not fully understand the depth of our own transgressions. True humility involves a deeper recognition of the divine love that humbles us—this is the love of Christ, who was crucified for sinners. As stated in Romans 5:8, "*But God demonstrates His own love toward us, in that while we were still sinners, Christ died for us.*"

True humility begins with accepting the image of a servant, reflecting the Lord Himself who embraced human servitude without complaint. He lived this role fully to redeem humanity. True humility starts by embracing this servant role and accepting our own place within it. It is not about confronting or becoming troubled by the pride of others but about resisting pride with love. We must avoid harbouring hidden pride that leads us to believe that we can renew others' lives through reprimand, threats, or public shaming. Such attitudes are symptoms of a deeper spiritual death within the heart.

A proud person, when they fall, is often shocked, regretful, and loses hope. In contrast, a humble person, who is aware of their own weaknesses, is not surprised by their own behaviour or shortcomings. They experience regret with a living hope in God's mercy and forgiveness.

Instead of asking God to grant you humility directly, seek from Him the revelation of the hidden secrets of your heart. Understanding these secrets will lead you to rely on the work of the Holy Spirit, as your weakness will continually remind you of the need for God's mercy and redemption.

If love—specifically, an understanding of God's love—is what cultivates humility, then humility itself is the seed of the kingdom. It grows into a magnificent tree, as Jesus described: *"The kingdom of God is like a mustard seed, which a man took and planted in his garden. It grew and became a tree, and the birds of the air perched in its branches"* (Luke. 13:19). This metaphor illustrates how genuine humility, like a small seed, has the potential to develop into something profoundly transformative and nurturing.

The Role of Confession in Spiritual Healing

When we struggle with a specific sin, it often reveals a deficiency in our love—both our self-love and our love for God. Therefore, true and acceptable confession involves acknowledging that we may love ourselves more than we love God.

If a particular sin is favoured over others and results in repeated falls, it indicates a deeper issue that requires the remedy of the cross. This involves crucifying the will through thoughtful reflection and subduing the body through practices like fasting and vigilance. These practices help to break our attachment to sin, but ultimate healing comes from the Holy Spirit.

Repeated confession of a specific sin should be addressed with three healing remedies:

1. *Act Contrary to the Sin*: This means cultivating a pure heart by rejecting what is good for the sake of God. Engage in acts of service to others, and maintain continual confession to God to foster genuine repentance.

2. *Pursue Celibacy of Heart*: This involves rejecting even what is good in the context of serving God, focusing on service to others, and maintaining an on-going, humble relationship with God.

3. *Commit to Regular Confession*: This consistent act reinforces the process of transformation and growth in humility.

Through love and sacrifice, we transition from the bondage of fear to the freedom of love through teaching. As we learn, we become disciples who are free from the anxieties of fear and the terror of hell. Human fear does not bring us closer to God. Instead, God, who approached us and became like us in every way except sin, draws us nearer.

Discerning the Intentions of the Heart

How, then, can we discern the true intentions of our hearts? The cross serves as our guiding principle, much like the helm of a ship directing its course. Thus, anything opposed to the crucified love, which rises from the sufferings of death and triumphs over the grave, should be judged immediately and without delay.

To discern the intentions of your heart, consider the following:

1. *Evaluate Your Goals*: Examine what you aim to achieve and determine if it aligns with the cross. Abandon anything that fosters enmity, hatred, and division, as the Lord has called us to unity. He urges us to go "the extra mile" and avoid disputes over temporary matters.

2. *Determine the Path*: Identify the path you should follow. Jesus is the only way, and your path and goal should be one of sacred unity. Evil does not produce good, lies do not serve truth, and immorality does not uphold chastity.

If Jesus is the way and the goal, He has summarized the essence of discernment in two key statements:

1. *"No one can serve two masters"* (Luke. 16:13). This means that one cannot be divided in their loyalties and still serve God faithfully.

2. *"Whoever does not deny himself and take up his cross and follow me is not worthy of me"* (Matt.16:24). This indicates that one must fully embrace the call to follow Jesus and

share in His sufferings to truly participate in His kingdom.

A person with a divided heart and tongue is no longer unified; they have become estranged even from their own body. Such a person behaves as if they do not recognize the boundaries between good and evil, mixing them as the ancient Israelites did when Elijah cried out, *"How long will you falter between two opinions?"* (1 Kg.18:21). A person with a divided heart is unsuitable for anything; they are like someone who has *"put his hand to the plow"* but looks back, as the Lord said. Looking back refers to the old past life that Jesus warned us against. New wine cannot be put into old wineskins, and a new patch cannot be added to an old garment (Luke. 5:36-37).

Reveal the intentions of your heart to the Lord Jesus, and let the Jesus Prayer be the beginning of every thought, word, and action. As you engage in prayer and fellowship, you will learn how to discern the true intentions of your heart and align them with God's will.

Living Under the Grace of Christ: Embracing True Purity and Understanding the Role of the Psalms

We are not bound by the strictures of the law, nor are we subject to the compulsion of Christ's teachings in a way that imposes burden or constraint. Jesus did not come into the world to be served but to serve and to offer His life as a ransom for many (Mark. 10:45). This fundamental truth signifies that Jesus Christ, our Savior, lives within us, not merely outside us. He is the Head of the Church, the Body of Christ, imparting spiritual life to every part of this body. Understanding this divine truth is crucial; otherwise, one may find themselves perplexed and disoriented in various aspects of life. This is why we turn to the Psalms—not only to safeguard ourselves from becoming overly absorbed in our personal and daily needs but also to ensure we continue to praise God alongside His creation and express our gratitude for the immense gift of salvation .The Psalms serve as our foundational school of repentance, a place where we must enter with discernment and a deep understanding to truly learn the core principles of our faith.

We should approach the Psalms with a spirit of humility and insight, particularly when encountering the more severe or curse-filled passages of the Psalms.

These passages reflect the ancient people's adherence to a law of retribution, where justice was often meted out according to the principle of *"an eye for an eye, and a tooth for a tooth"* (Matt.5:38). However, it is important to recognize that we do not reject these Psalms outright. Instead, we should read them in conjunction with passages that recount the historical battles of the Israelites and their struggle against idolatry. It is not necessary to recite these Psalms verbatim, such as Psalm 35, if they do not resonate with our current spiritual experience. The Church, guided by the Holy Spirit's wisdom, has carefully arranged the Psalms to be read before the Gospel to aid in our repentance and to seek the Lord's grace and assistance. Sometimes, we combine excerpts from different Psalms before reading the Gospel to illustrate that we are learning the art of supplication, intercession, and petition in the primary school of prayer—the Book of Psalms.

For those who find pleasure or justification in invoking the downfall of their enemies, supported by certain Psalms, they may unknowingly align themselves with the mind-set of the ancient people. They may fail to recognize that, as members of the Body of Christ, we are called to emulate Christ's forgiveness. Christ forgave those who crucified Him, and it is crucial to understand the distinction between the old and new covenants. Moses was a servant within God's house, but Jesus Christ is the Master of the house (Heb.3:3-6). We are not establishing new laws but adhering to the teachings of our faith as our ultimate guide.

It is said of the Lord Jesus that "*When He was reviled, He did not revile in return; when He suffered, He did not threaten, but committed Himself to Him who judges righteously*" (1 Peter. 2:23). God's justice has the power to restore those who have fallen. The Lord did not pronounce curses upon the Israelites; rather, He cursed the fig tree as a visible symbol of judgment while still allowing time for repentance. Similarly, we are called to follow "*the bond of perfection*" (Col.3:14), which is love. The Lord instructs us to "*bless those who curse you*" (Matt. 5:44), and this principle should guide us in our prayers, seeking blessings for everyone we encounter.

It is important to distinguish between physical cleanliness and purity of heart. While maintaining physical cleanliness is commendable, a grand tomb can still house dead bones. Our focus should not be on specific customs or laws regarding bodily cleanliness, as these fall under the personal responsibility of each believer in Christ. Through the sacrament of baptism, we are purified, and our on-going need is to cleanse ourselves from dead works through repentance. The waters of creation do not draw us closer to God; rather, it is through repentance that we attain spiritual purity.

In conclusion, we must constantly remind ourselves that Christ is our eternal life, a life that transcends the reach of death. This is why we honour the Holy Gospel in our prayers, for it symbolizes joy and life. The Gospel reassures us that our repentance preserves what we have received and does not bestow additional grace. The fullness of grace is found in Jesus Christ Himself, and through Him, we repent to become participants in His heavenly inheritance. To Him be glory with the Father and the Holy Spirit, forever and ever. Amen.

LOGOS ECHOES
WHEREVER LOGOS INSPIRE

Welcome To The Realm Of Logos

Where the profound realms of theology and spirituality intertwine, your journey of faith begins. Embark on a transformative quest for knowledge and spiritual growth as we offer a rich tapestry of E-books designed to nourish your soul and ignite your mind.

At the heart of Logos Echoes beats a passion for sharing the life-changing power of God's Word. We illuminate the timeless truths of Christianity with a fresh perspective, providing a captivating blend of deep theological insights and practical wisdom. By understanding the heart of God and the mind of Christ, we empower believers to live out their faith with confidence and purpose.

Our ministry is to ignite a flame within your heart, deepening your connection with Christ and equipping you to share His love with the world. Discover thought-provoking insights, practical guidance, and timeless truths that will transform your life, Through the life-changing message of Jesus Christ.

Together, we will unlock the boundless potential of your faith and experience the profound peace and fulfilment found in a deep relationship with Christ.

Waiting To Hear From You

If you find it worth it, please don't hesitate to contact us. Your feedback is like gold to us! These insights help us improve, grow, and create better Christian content for everyone. Share your thoughts and ideas with us. You are always welcome. And remember, our goal is:

**TOGETHER WITH LOGOS,
WE MAKE THE WORLD BETTER**

Email us: logosechoes@gmail.com

About the Author

Sameh Saied is A Researcher and Self-Published Author in the Field of Christian Studies, Particularly Focusing on the History of Early Christianity ,also the Founder of Logos Echoes Publications. His Aim is to Publish Works that address Theological, Biblical, and Spiritual Topics of interest to readers, to foster a deeper understanding of the Christian Faith, which is reflected in individual lives and society as a whole, by presenting diverse perspectives on the Bible and Christian Doctrines. Until now published four books:

- God Among Us: The Rational Case for the Incarnation.

- The Heart of Jesus: Unveiling His Eternal Love for Humanity.

- Restoring the Divine Participation: The Holy Spirit's Role and the Path to True Repentance.

- Recreating Humanity: Illuminating Our Divine Identity in Christ.

Copyright © LOGOS ECHOES PUBLICATIONS

www.ingramcontent.com/pod-product-compliance
Lightning Source LLC
Chambersburg PA
CBHW071442130726
47997CB00006B/2192